Figure it out!

think your way to skating great figures

12 - 25-92

Nina Stark-Slapnik

*Happy Figure Skating
Emmie!
Merry Christmas dear!!
Love,
Dad & mom*

Graphic Design by
Jo-Ann Dontenville

Artwork and Cover Design by
Cheryl Broomfield Onesky

Professional Skaters Guild of America
P.O. Box 5904
Rochester, MN 55903

To Bob,

for believing in my idea,
for supporting me in all phases of production and
for being the greatest guy!

1st printing 1986
2nd printing 1987
3rd printing 1992

ISBN #0-9616977-0 9

Published simultaneously in the United States and Canada
Printed in the United States of America

Table of Contents

Acknowledgements

I'd like to recognize some of the many people who were instrumental in helping me complete this project. Jo-Ann Dontenville is responsible for the appearance and layout of this book. The editorial comments of Susan Terkel, Adele Stark, and Bob Slapnik helped establish the structure and content of this book.

Special thanks go to Dale Mitch at the USFSA and Carole Shulman of the PSGA for assisting me in gathering small details; to Cheryl Broomfield Onesky for the artwork on the front cover and the lesson pages; to Kim Cool, Christie Haigler Krall, Bev Keller, Michael Masionis, Betty Palascak, and especially Bill Spiegelberg for reading the manuscript and offering valuable suggestions; to everyone at Coyle Graphics; and to each of the National, World, and Olympic Champions who responded with photos and/or comments: Peggy Fleming, Janet Lynn, Scott Hamilton and Rosalynn Sumners. I'd like to express my deep appreciation to Robin Cousins who graciously gave his time and energy to support this project: he is as charming off the ice as he is on the ice.

I am grateful to all of my students of the past 15 years who participated in this book by helping me to clearly formulate my ideas.

I am honored to receive the PSGA Seal of Approval. I thank the members of the PSGA, its Board of Directors, and especially the Technical Committee, Kathy Casey, Bob Crowley, and Pieter Kollen for their support.

I'd like to acknowledge all the new and renewed friends I have made as a result of this endeavor.

Lastly, I'd like to thank my mother, father, brothers and sisters for making it possible for me to skate to my hearts content!

Introduction

If you are one of those people who was always told figures are boring, do I have news for you! When I saw this book, my first reaction was ... "Where was this when I needed it fifteen years ago!!" Now you have the opportunity to learn AND have fun with figures.

No one can tell you better than I how important figures are in the basic structure of your skating style. I may not have been the greatest compulsory figures' skater in the world, but without the groundwork I had at Novice levels, I would never have won the Olympics.

This book now gives you the chance to be one skate ahead of the rest. So, grab your pencil and start drawing. I'm sure you'll find that you can't wait to go to the rink, try your new skills, and dare I say it....*SKATE CIRCLES 'ROUND YOUR FRIENDS!!*

Robin Cousins

Robin Cousins GBR. 1980 Olympic Champion
photo AP/Wide World Photos

Message to Skaters:

Do you want your compulsory figures to get better? Of course! That's why you spend three or four times a day practicing figures. Improving your figures can sometimes feel painstakingly slow. Even champion skaters find that skating good figures requires concentration and precision - qualities that take time to learn. If only there were other ways to improve besides spending hours on the ice. Now there is a new way to practice figures: on paper and in your mind. That's what we do in *FIGURE IT OUT*:   teach you to draw figures on paper with precision and to picture them in your mind through visualization. Your blade cuts a picture on the ice just as your pencil draws an image on paper. When the figures you draw on paper improve, so do the figures you cut on the ice.

With this workbook, a well sharpened pencil, a pair of scissors, and a compass, you will 1) refine your mental image of circles, 2) draw better circles on paper and on ice, and 3) learn to layout circles on clean ice. For greatest success, follow the exercises in the order given. Expect to complete two lessons per week.

As your mental picture of circles improves, so will your figures. Won't you, your coach, and your parents be pleased if you progress faster on tests and place higher in competitions? You bet! So have fun with this workbook. When you are finished, send us the form at the end of the book with your coach's signature. We'll send you a diploma with your name inscribed on it! *Good Luck !*

Message to Parents:

Does your child dislike figures? Many skaters don't like figures because their minds are inactive during patch. *FIGURE IT OUT* gives them something to think about - the blueprint of the figure they are trying to draw on the ice.

The exercises are written for skaters of all ages and all levels. They provide a great foundation for low testers and are even valuable for high testers. Skaters age eight or younger may need adult supervision.

Clean ice for figures is expensive and sometimes hard to find. Certainly it is difficult to arrange enough lesson time with your coach. Although *FIGURE IT OUT* is not meant to replace ice time or lessons, it is meant to supplement them. Going through the exercises frequently and in the order provided will accelerate your child's learning on the ice.

As your child's mental picture of figures improves, so will his/her figures. Working through *FIGURE IT OUT* can make time spent on the ice more productive, helping your child to progress faster and place higher in competitions. Encourage your child to complete the entire book over several months (two lessons per week). Apply for a diploma by returning the form at the end of the workbook. We'll send a diploma - a fine measure of success.

Message to Coaches:

If you, your student, and a high level judge were to stand back to review a figure on the ice, would each of you see the same things? Probably not. Teaching figures requires that you teach your students to see subtleties that they never even imagined. This process of learning to "see" usually involves learning to step back and look at the overview of the figure. Years of teaching experience have shown that this can easily be done on paper. *FIGURE IT OUT* has evolved from a series of off ice figure drawing classes based on the principle that the figure you draw on paper resembles the one you cut on the ice.

These exercises were developed to help skaters understand the geometry of circles and to give them a blueprint of what the figure should look like. If the skater has a clear, precise picture in his/her mind of what they are trying to achieve, it helps them to produce better results on the ice. Furthermore, in *FIGURE IT OUT* skaters learn to see and rank mistakes.

FIGURE IT OUT is not meant to be a technique for skating figures. Instead, it explains complex principles of the physics of circles in a language that children can understand. After these lessons, a skater feels empowered to skate good figures because he knows them better. The exercises in *FIGURE IT OUT* actively involve the skater in a learning experience over several months. Plan on students completing two lessons per week. Students progress through the *FIGURE IT OUT* program on their own or with your help. In either case the results are terrific!

To maintain the value of the diploma we offer, please review your skater's work before signing the diploma application at the end of the book. Feel free to include any comments, questions, or suggestions with the form.

LESSON

1

Concepts

We're off! First you must answer an important question. Why are circles important in your patch? Because patch is simply a series of circles. Let's see how good you are at drawing circles. In one smooth motion, try your hand at drawing a circle in the space below.

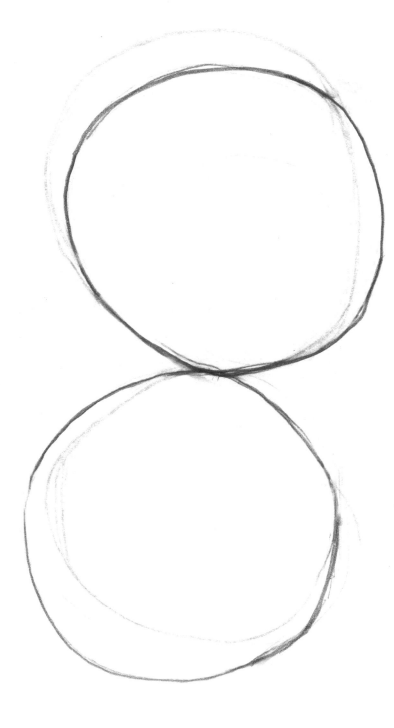

Look at your circle.

Is it round? Chances are it isn't perfectly round. Now, draw a second circle directly below the first one. Try to make it the same size as the first one.

Look how hard it was to draw a good circle. It's even harder to draw a second one exactly the same size and shape as the first one, isn't it?

If this is hard to do on paper, just imagine how hard it is when you are drawing with your feet on the ice!

Now we're going to make it easier to draw a circle by giving you two lines. This time draw a circle inside the two lines shown below. Start on the line. Judge the size of the circle so it barely touches each line.

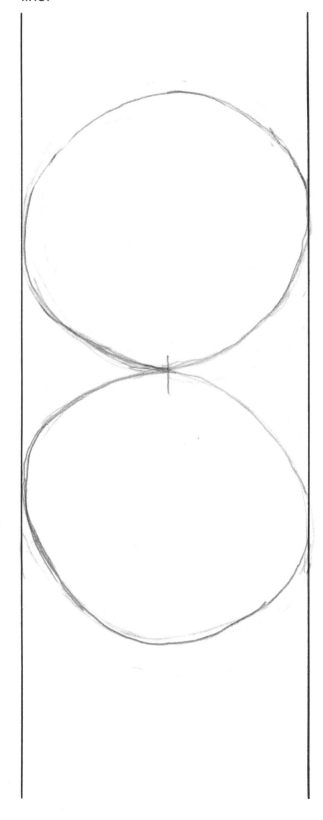

Look at your circle. Was it easier? Was your circle better than the ones you drew on the first page without the lines? Most likely it was easier and better. Did you move your hand evenly and smoothly? You should always try to draw your circle in one continuous and even motion. Since you want to skate your figures in a smooth, even, free-flowing manner, try to move your hand and pencil in the same way.

Try drawing a second circle below the first one. Again, start on the line, move your hand freely and glide your pencil continuously across the paper. Did the two lines make it easier to draw the second circle to match the first one in shape and size?
Probably.

Do you recognize these two lines? They are the **SIDE LINES** of your patch. The side lines keep the edges of your circles even so you don't skate on your neighbor's patch.

The side lines marking your patch are **PARALLEL LINES**. What is unique about two lines that are parallel? Well, parallel lines are two lines on the same surface that never meet no matter how long they are extended. At all points, parallel lines are the same distance apart. Parallel lines look like this ‖ or this ═══ or this ⫽ .

The side runners of a ladder are parallel to each other. The top of the dinner table is parallel to the floor, because if it were slanted everything would fall off. In the rink, the side lines of your patch are parallel to the hockey lines. Although the side lines of your patch never meet each other, they do meet the boards of the ice rink. In fact the side lines of your patch are always perpendicular ⊥ to the boards. Look at the picture below.

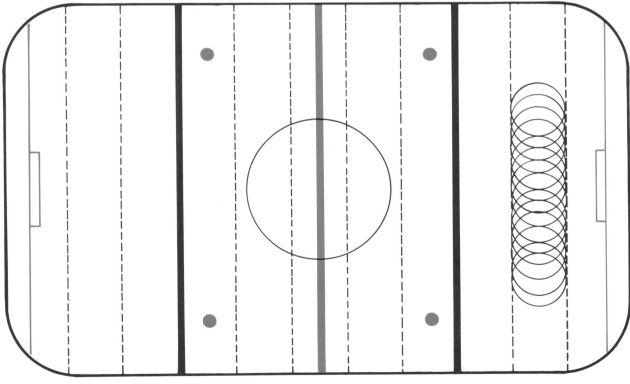

THE RINK

PERPENDICULAR LINES meet each other at right angles and look like this:⌐

or this ⌐   or this ∟

The steps of the ladder are perpendicular to the side runners of the ladder. The legs of the table are perpendicular to the top of the table. Unless the table is round, the corners of the table form right angles. The lines below are not perpendicular to each other:

Can you see how the space or angle between each set of two lines is not a square?

Perpendicular lines are always at the same right or square angle to each other. Perpendicular lines meet and sometimes cross like this: ┼ .

Look around you and list five objects that have perpendicular parts:

Window _____   Pitcher frame   Box _____

garbige top _____   Changing table _____

Draw One:

List five objects that have parallel sides:

Changing table   crib _____   lines in wood

window _____   Wall paper disines

Draw One:

Circle all the sets of lines that are not parallel

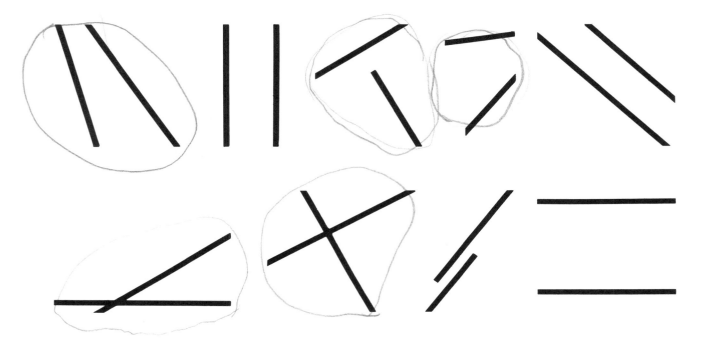

Circle any set of lines that are not perpendicular

see bottom of p. 56 for answers

At the end of patch one day stand back and look at the patches where everyone skated. You can tell how good a skater is by how neat their patch is. A good skater's patch looks like the one drawn on the left below: each circle is distinct and no tracings stick out over the side lines of the patch. Even though they don't usually have to draw the side lines on the ice, advanced skaters cut their circles so neatly that the side lines of their patch are neat, straight, and perpendicular to the side boards.

The picture below is a beginner's patch. See how the tracings stick out on the side? This makes the side lines look ragged. Also notice how the circles don't stand out distinctly. The exercises in this book will help you to skate a patch like the one on the left.

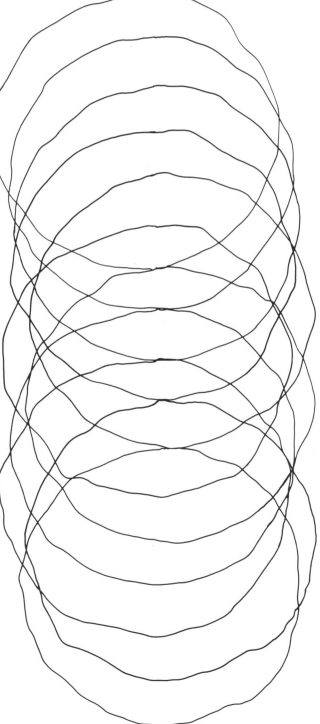

Just as the tracks of a train keep the wheels of the train in line, the side lines of your patch keep your circles in line with each other. When your circles are **LINED UP**, each circle is in line with the other and measures the same width. If the widest parts of the circle are on a line parallel to the patch line, then the sides are lined up. When skating, imagine that the side lines of your patch are really part of an electric fence: if you skate over the line you will feel an electric zap.

Lined up circles look like this: Circles that are not lined up look like this:

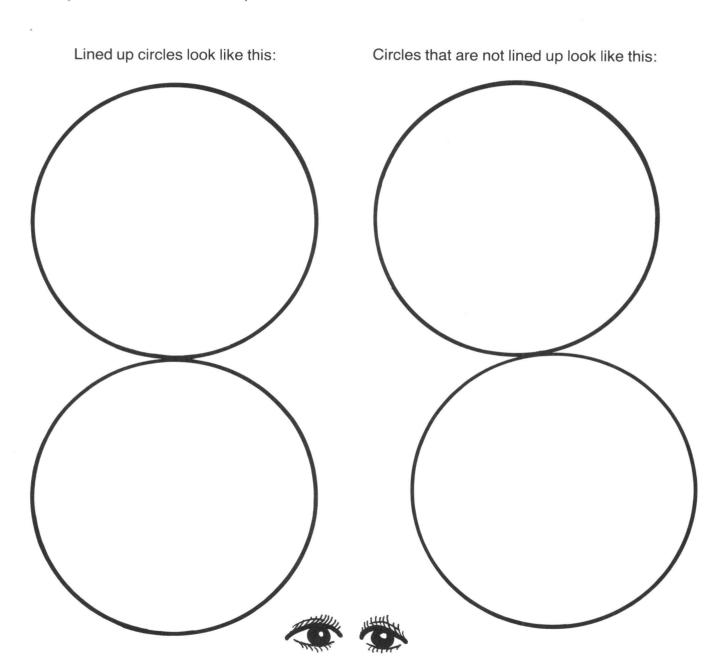

CAN YOU SEE THE DIFFERENCE?

The circles drawn on the left are lined up with the page: if you draw a line to connect the sides of these circles, this line is parallel to the sides of the paper. Use your ruler and do this now. Do the same thing for the circles on the right. Notice how the circles on the left line up parallel to the page, while the circles on the right do not. This page is the same shape as your patch on the ice.

Now that you are familiar with the concepts of parallel and perpendicular lines, let's examine one more concept before advancing to the next lesson: the difference between turning **CLOCKWISE** or **COUNTERCLOCKWISE.**

Stand up and turn around once. Which way did you turn, to the right or left? Good. You only had two choices, so now turn the opposite direction.

Now you have turned to the right looking over your right shoulder, and you have turned left looking over your left shoulder.

Turning to the right goes this way:

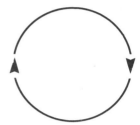

This is also called turning clockwise because the hands of the clock turn to the right (as you face the clock).

When you turn to the left you turn this way:

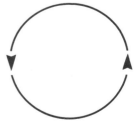

This is called turning counterclockwise or the opposite direction of the clock (as you face the clock).

When you skate a figure eight on the ice, one circle always turns clockwise and one circle turns counterclockwise. For this reason, you are going to practice drawing circles in both directions throughout this book.

EDGES

The groove along the length of your blade creates two **EDGES** - an **INSIDE** edge and an **OUTSIDE** one. If your foot is completely flat to the ice or straight over the blade, then both edges are touching the ice. The path you skate will be straight and the mark left on the ice will be two parallel lines ⅛ inch (.32 cms.) apart called a **FLAT** (see the picture).

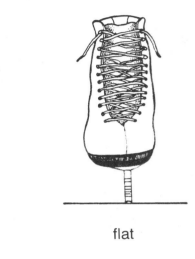

flat

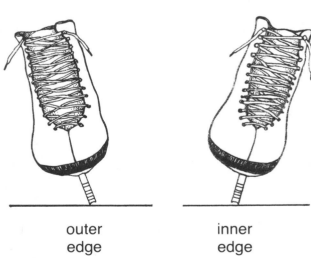

outer edge   inner edge

When your right foot leans towards the outside of your leg, you will curve to the right and skate an outer edge. When your right foot rolls and tilts towards the inside of your leg, you will curve to the left and skate an inner edge. The tilt of your blade creates a curve and an edge.

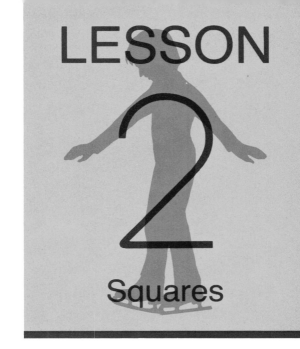

So you want to draw better circles? Then you have to understand squares. You're probably thinking, "Why should I care about squares? I have to skate circles!" You see, circles fit neatly inside of squares. Furthermore, after knowing the qualities that make a square unique, you will understand what makes circles different from other round shapes. When you can see a square in your mind, you will picture and skate better circles.

How do you make a square? Below is a grid of dots. Starting with your pencil on the red dot, draw a line to the right across the page connecting six more dots. From the last dot on the right, connect six more dots straight down in a line perpendicular to the first line. Now, turn a corner and move across to the left connecting six more dots. This line is parallel to the first line and perpendicular to the second line. Finally, draw a line straight up to the first red dot.

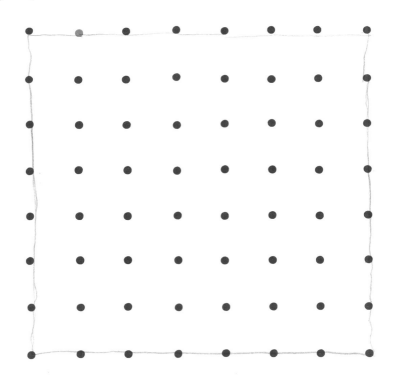

Have you made a square? Here is how to check. How many dots are on each side of your square? ___8___ If you said seven you are right. If your shape doesn't have the same number of dots on each side, it isn't a square. Instead, it might be a rectangle. All four sides of a square are equal in length. Are the corners perpendicular? _Yes_ They should be. Is each side parallel to the opposite side? _yes_ If you drew a square, then the answer to both these questions will be yes.

Both rectangles and squares have parallel sides and perpendicular corners. These common qualities make them brother and sisters. Then, how is a rectangle different from a square? A rectangle has two parallel sides longer than the other two sides. Rectangles can look like this [ ] or like this [ ]. In the first case the *width* is longer than the *length*.

In the second case, which is longer, (circle one) the   width   or the   length?   If you circled the length you were right.

Since we live in three-dimensional rectangles and squares, we are familiar with rectangular shapes. How many people do you know who live in round houses? Not many do. Is your house a perfect square or a rectangle? *rectangle*

A square is a special type of rectangle because all sides are equal. A square has three special qualities: **1)** all four corners are alike and perpendicular, **2)** opposite sides of the square are parallel, and **3)** all the sides are equal in length.

Circle all the shapes below **except** the squares.

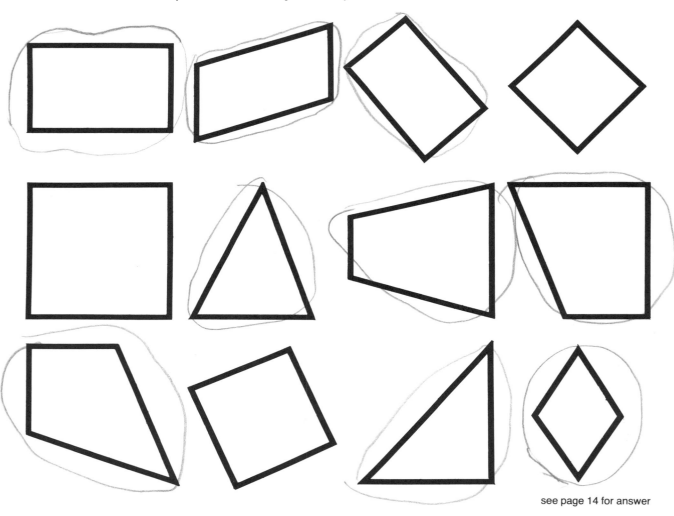

see page 14 for answer

A square is unusual because it is as wide as it is long. **Circles fit into squares** because **circles are as long as they are wide.**

If circles fit into squares then ...

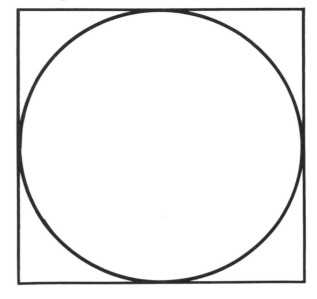

...What round shape fits into a rectangle?

(an oval or an ellipse)

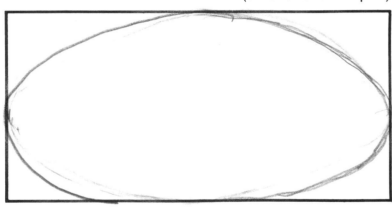

DRAW IT

Have you ever skated ovals instead of circles? Of course you have! Ovals are longer than they are wide. Or, ovals can be wider than they are long!
Draw an oval in each of the shapes below. These ovals are leaning to one side.

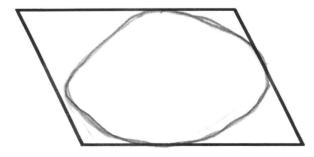

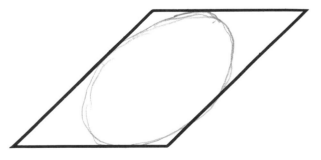

You've probably skated these distorted leaning ovals too! Judges deduct points from your figure if the circles you skate are really ovals. If the ovals you skated are leaning to either side of the long axis, then the judges deduct even more points from your score.

Fruits and vegetables come in many different sizes and shapes. What fruits and vegetables are longer than they are wide, like ovals? *Draw some below.*

egg

tomato

pumpkin

strawberry

watermelon

Can you think of a fruit that is most like a circle? *Draw it.*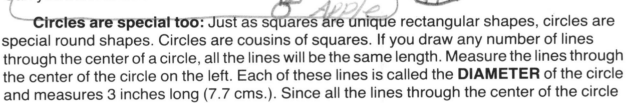

Circles are special too: Just as squares are unique rectangular shapes, circles are special round shapes. Circles are cousins of squares. If you draw any number of lines through the center of a circle, all the lines will be the same length. Measure the lines through the center of the circle on the left. Each of these lines is called the **DIAMETER** of the circle and measures 3 inches long (7.7 cms.). Since all the lines through the center of the circle are equal, the width and length of the circle are each a diameter of the circle.

On the right the circle rests inside of a square. How long is each side of the square? Again, each side of the square measures the same length as any diameter of the circle. Knowing this will help you to judge the size and shape of your circle on the ice.

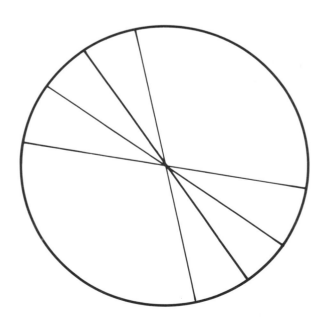

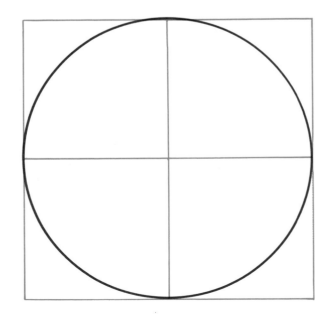

QUIZ LESSONS 1 and 2

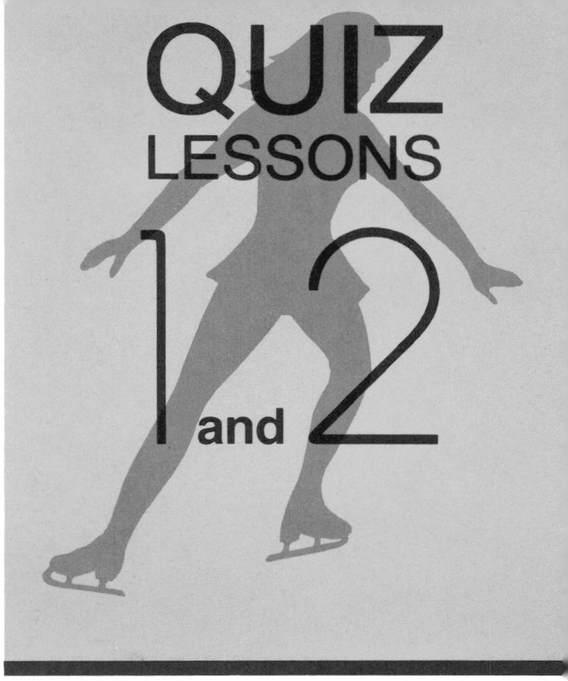

1. What round shape fits into a square?

circle

2. What round shape fits into a rectangle where two sides are longer than the other two sides?

Ovil

3. What are the lines called that go through the center of a circle?

dieamaters

4. When a circle is drawn inside a square and fills the square exactly, how many times do the circle and the square touch each other?

four times

5. Name two geometric shapes that are as long as they are wide?

Sqare circle

6. Describe what it means when two lines are parallel? No mater how long Palallel never tock.

Draw two parallel lines.

7. Define perpendicular lines. Angles meeting on the right.

Draw two perpendicular lines.

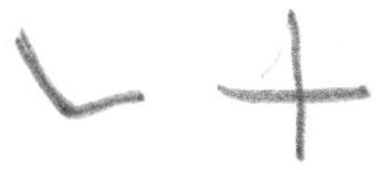

turn page for answers

HISTORY OF FIGURES

Skating as an art and sport really began when skaters became fascinated by the designs they could draw on the ice with their blades. In 1870 the metal blade was grooved for the first time. This created edges which gave the skater greater freedom in creating designs. For centuries every movement, turn, or leap created on the ice were called figures based on the print left on the ice. The distinction between free style and figures evolved in the 1860's from contests between various skating clubs in Europe, especially the Vienna Skating Club in Austria. The famous American skater Jackson Haines visited Vienna in 1864-65 and greatly stimulated the development of both figures and freestyle.

The idea in Vienna was to create prescribed or "school" figures out of fundamental skating elements, much like a mathematical problem. The goal was to create a logical consistancy through all the figures so there would be harmony. By the late 1860's all the turns like threes, brackets, counters, and rockers were skated on circles about 10 feet in diameter. Circles were skated with the stepdowns crossed and the pushes were open. It wasn't until 1927 that Centers were skated geometrically correct as they are today.

In 1882 the first international skating meeting convened and specified that 23 figures, one "special" figure, and a four minute freestyle program would be performed at competitions. Dr. C. Korper spearheaded the formation of the ISU (International Skating Union) in 1892, the definition of the 64 figures, and the scoring system we know today. The first World Figure Skating Competition was held in 1896. Beside school figures and freestyle, each skater performed a "special" figure: these were done on small circles and required great swings of the free leg and bending of the skating knee. The lack of toe picks and the great rock of the blade made it possible to do these figures which consisted of beaks, crosscuts, spectacles and anvils as pictured below:

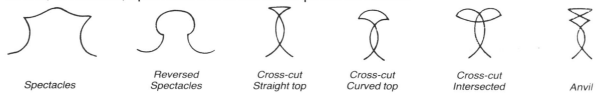

| Spectacles | Reversed Spectacles | Cross-cut Straight top | Cross-cut Curved top | Cross-cut Intersected | Anvil |

These complicated turns were put together to create "special" figures like the following ones skated at Worlds in 1896.

QUIZ ANSWERS
LESSONS 1 & 2

1. a circle
2. oval
3. diameters
4. four
5. square, circle
6. no matter how long they are, parallel lines never meet.

7. they cross at right angles.

answers from page 10

Circle all the shapes below *except* the squares.

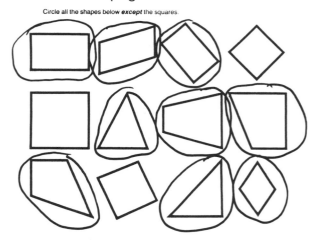

Let's begin to explore the relationship between circles and squares. Below on the left you see two squares each with a perfect circle drawn inside. Trace each circle 15 times in the direction indicated. Let your hand move freely, smoothly and evenly.

Clockwise

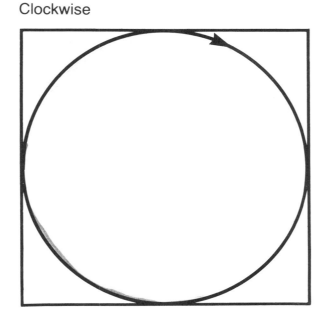

Counterclockwise

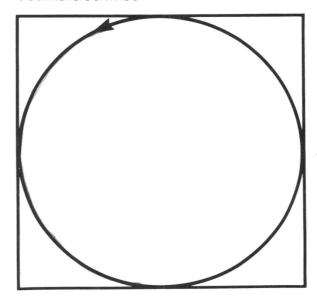

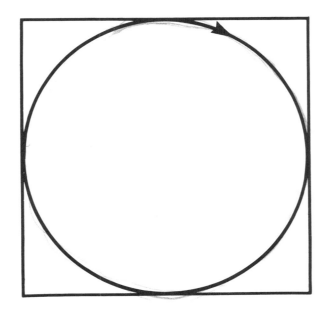

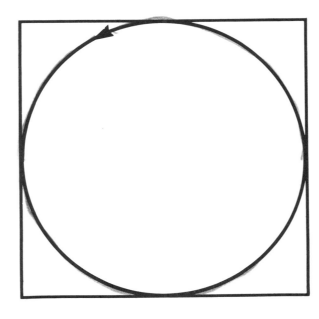

Notice the four points where the circle touches the square. Now in the squares to the right draw around each circle 15 times in the other direction.

See if you can draw the circle on your own inside each square. Use the four points as guidelines. Imagine how each circle fits into and just touches the square at the four points. Try several times to draw your circle until you are satisfied with the results.

Clockwise

Counterclockwise

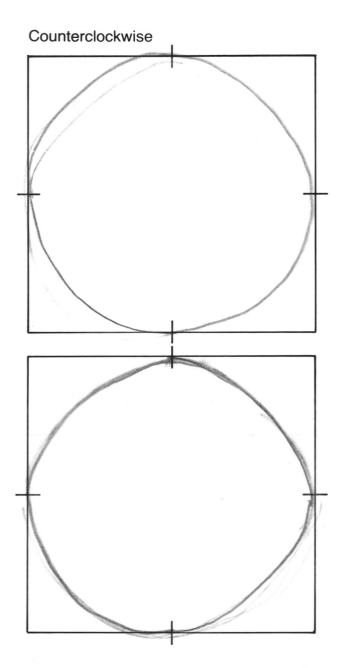

How did you do? Are your shapes round or oval? Look on the previous page to remind yourself what the circle looks like in the square.

Now the real fun begins: grab your scissors and cut out all the squares below. One at a time cut a circle out of each square (without any folding). Compare your circle to the one we have drawn inside the circle below. Look at the circles you just cut out. Each one probably has a few dents and bulges. Your coach might call those wobbles or **SUBCURVES** if you skated a circle like that on the ice. Your skate cuts a geometric figure out of the ice just as your scissors cut a circle out of the paper. You have to know in your mind the shapes of a circle and a square to cut better figures on the ice.

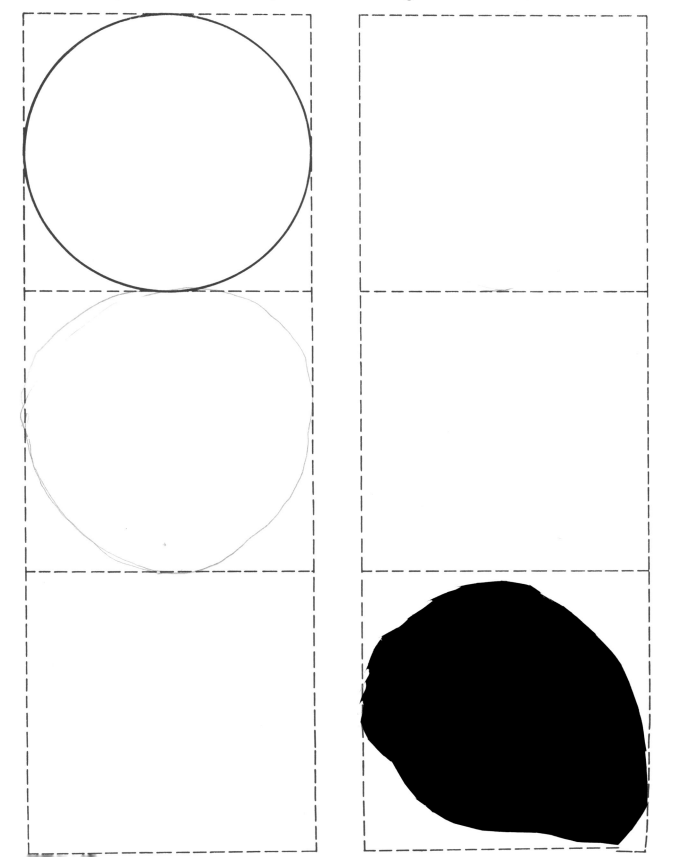

Cut out the squares below along the dotted lines. Notice that each square on this page has two perpendicular lines drawn across it. These lines cut the square into four equal parts which are also squares. If a circle were cut out of the square as before, your scissors would touch the square in the same four points as the lines do. Cut circles out of the squares beginning with the circle already drawn.

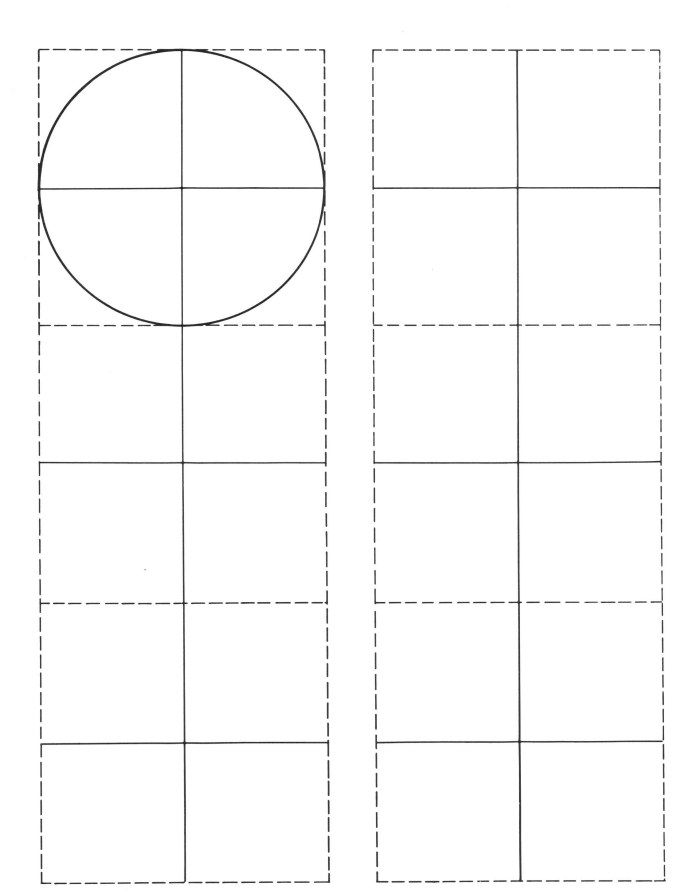

Before proceeding, you must understand the concepts of **LONG AXIS** and **SHORT AXIS**. During patch your coach talks about the **LONG AXIS** which divides each circle in half into two matching pieces. The long axis runs down the length of BOTH circles of a figure eight and lines up the first circle with the second one. It cuts each circle in half and into two segments. Any segment of a circle is called an **ARC**.

The long axis cuts through the circle at two places: one at the **CENTER** where you change feet, and the other is at the top of the circle. If you follow the arc from the Center to the top of the circle, you have drawn half the circle. The spot at the top of the circle is called the **HALF**. Look at the figure drawn to see where the half is marked on each circle. The arc on the other side of the long axis matches the first side in size and shape.

Now that the circle is divided in half, we are going to divide it again to get four equal arcs by drawing several **SHORT AXIS** lines. The short axis is any shorter line perpendicular to the long axis. The most commonly discussed short axis runs through the Center of the figure (where you change feet) and separates the two circles from each other.

But there are many **"HIDDEN"** short axis lines on each circle. Can you guess where they are? Turn the page and you will see.

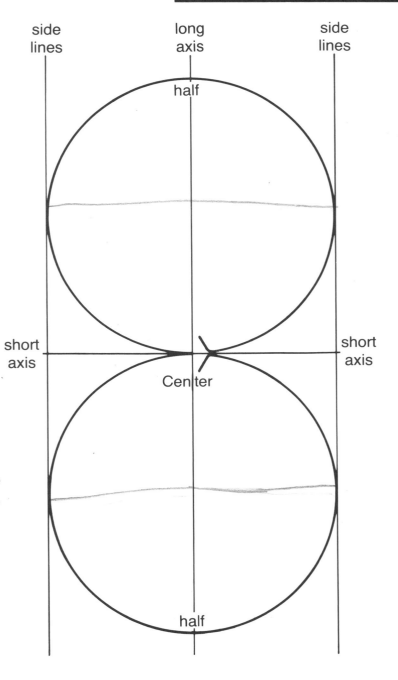

The **HIDDEN** short axis lines are shown as dotted lines in the picture to the right. These *hidden* lines actually finish a square around each circle. While the long axis cuts the circle into two matching arcs, the *hidden* short axis lines divide the square and the circle into four equal parts. If you start at the Center where the long and short axis cross and skate to the first *hidden* short axis, you have cut ¼ of the circle. For this reason, we call this point the 1st QUARTER. The **half** could also be called the 2nd QUARTER, and the 3rd QUARTER is marked as shown. The 4th QUARTER is the Center. These four equal parts are labeled in the drawing as 1st, 2nd, 3rd and 4th QUARTERS in the order they are skated.

Notice that the quarters of the circle are on the side lines in the figure drawn. When the widest points of the circle rest on the side lines, two circles are lined up with each other. When circles are lined up, both circles are on the same long axis and share the same side lines. Judges always stand at the edge of the figure to see if each side of each circle is lined up.

It is important to memorize how the circle fits into the corner of the square. Examine the first arc of the circle in one of the squares on the right. Look at the shaded space between the circle and the corner of the square. Does the circle curve into the corner of the square? Not really.

Take your ruler and draw a straight line between the Center and the 1st quarter. Good. A straight line is the shortest distance between the two points. Now imagine that you are standing at the Center about to skate this figure. Your eyes look along that straight line to the 1st quarter of the circle, don't they? But, you don't want to skate on that line. You don't want to skate into the corner either. The true circle falls somewhere in between these two extremes, and gradually curves to the quarter.

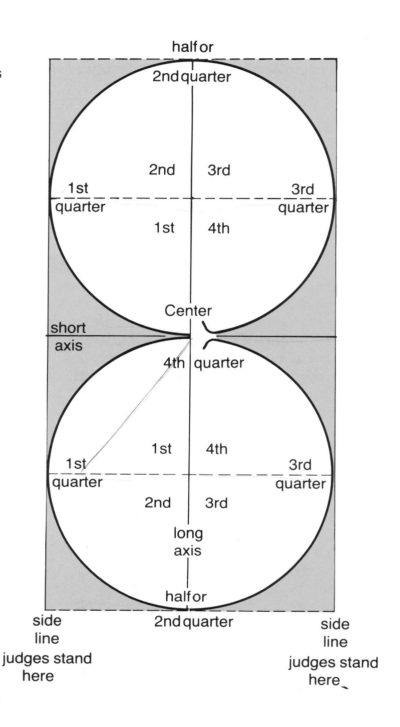

A forward outside eight is drawn inside the squares below on the left. With a flowing hand, trace the entire figure 15 times as you would skate it: include the pushes as part of the circle you are drawing. When you are done, draw the forward inside eight (on the right) by tracing 15 times on each circle. TRY TO PICTURE EACH QUARTER ARC IN YOUR MIND AS YOU TRACE EACH CIRCLE.

Forward Outside Eight

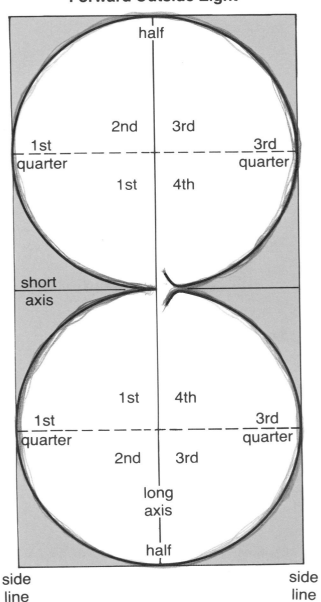

Forward Inside Eight

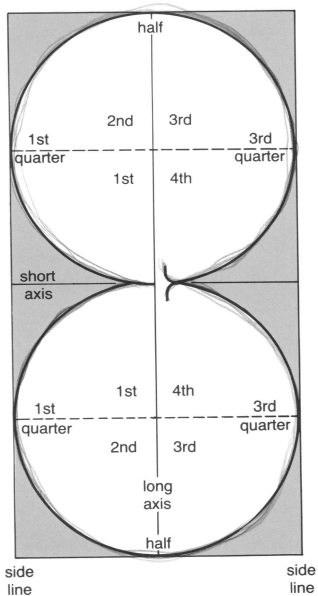

Now hold the picture of each arc in your mind and draw your own forward outside eight and forward inside eight inside of the squares.

Label the solid lines drawn on each figure and the special points on each circle.

HINT: there are six lines and six special points to be labeled on each figure. Check the previous page when you are done to see if you are correct.

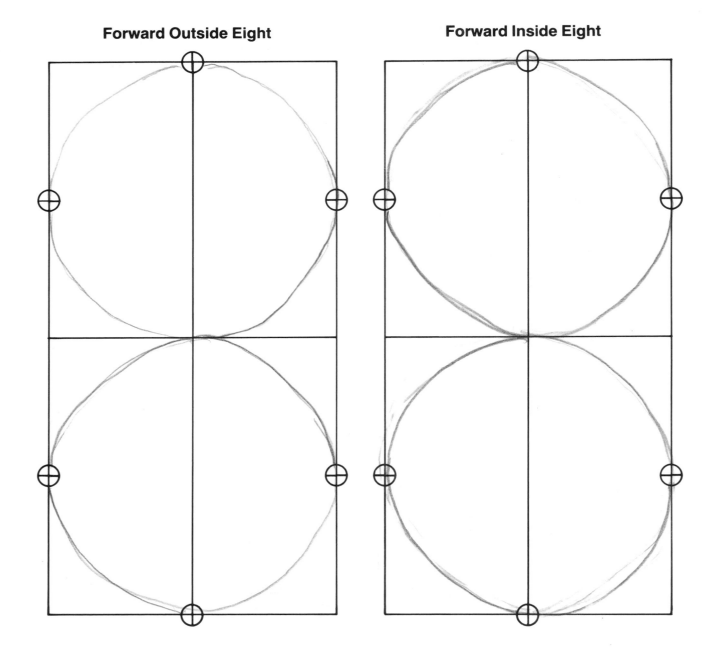

Forward Outside Eight   **Forward Inside Eight**

STAND UP and FACE THE WALL in the room where you are working. Now, walk a square. Start by taking two steps towards the first wall, then turning ¼ turn to the right. As you face the next wall, continue with two more steps and another ¼ rotation in the same direction. Pause as you face each wall and continue until completing a square and one revolution. This is what you do while gliding around a circle: you turn around once. Unlike the square, the rotation during a circle is so evenly spaced and continuous that you hardly notice you are turning.

As you walked the square, you faced in four directions. In relation to this page they are 1) left across, 2) up, 3) right across, and 4) down. Skating a circle requires moving in a combination of all these directions, except at the quarters and the halves where the circle touches the square. The direction of the circle at each of these four points is the same as the four directions of the square. See the picture below.

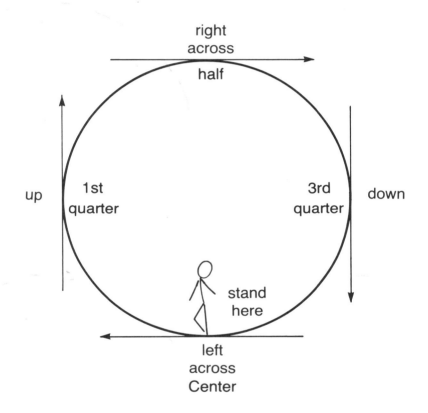

Now, imagine that you are standing at your Center about to *skate* a **R**ight **F**orward **O**utside eight (RFO). Because you are on the bottom edge of the square, your blade is aimed "left across". As you skate the circle, your body slowly turns ¼ rotation. When skating through the 1st quarter, for an instant your direction is completely "up" the side of the square. Again, turn ¼ rotation until passing the half, and notice how for a split second your blade points "right across". When you arrive at the 3rd quarter, you have made another ¼ rotation and are momentarily aiming "down" the side of the square. You finish the rotation as you skate back into your Center and again face "left across". Because the sides of the square indicate the direction at the quarters and the halves, it is clear where you are aiming at these four points. But what about the directions you face when skating the circle between the quarters and the halves? To answer this question you have to divide the circle into eight pieces. Turn the page and see.

The circle on the left below is divided into eight pieces. Count them and number them on the picture.

Just like the quarters and the halves, the eighths are special points on the circle. The eighth is exactly halfway between the quarter and the half on the arc of the circle.

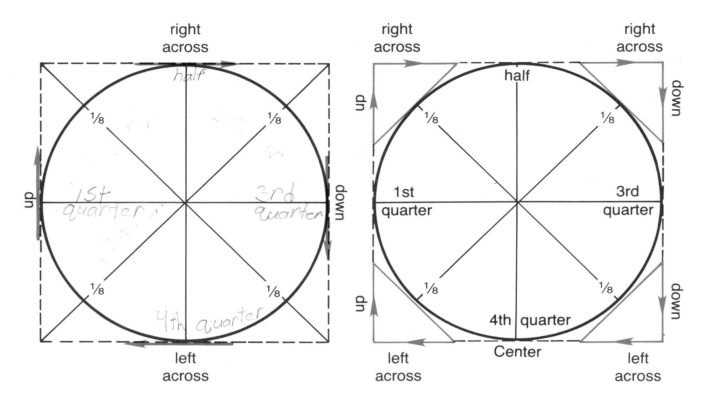

Imagine you are skating a right forward outside eight again. When skating through the eighth of the circle, besides being halfway between the widest and longest points of the circle, there is something "halfway" about the direction you face. Let's explain. Look at the circle above on the right. Imagine you are skating from the 1st quarter to the half of the circle. At the 1st quarter you are momentarily aiming "up" the side line and in no other direction. As you move towards the eighth, you still skate "up" but you begin to increase the amount of movement "across" to the right. At the eighth you are moving "up" exactly as much as you are moving "across". So, the "up" direction and the "across" direction are equal at this point. Then continuing your movement to the half, you gradually *increase* the amount of movement "across" to the right, as you gradually *decrease* the amount of movement "up". Arriving at the half, you are only moving "across" to the right and not "up" at all. This decreasing and increasing of directions happens all around the circle.

Skating good circles requires that you understand how the directions change while cutting a circular path between point A and point B. In these illustrations the true circle is shown by a dotted line in red. Imagine that the skater bulged the circle between the 1st quarter and the half as shown in the picture below:

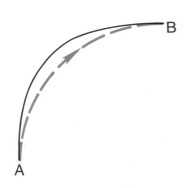

Can you see how he skated "up" the side line too long before starting "right across".

The next illustration on the right shows the mistake of bulging out in the 3rd quarter of the circle. The skater aimed "right across" too long and should have begun to turn "down" the side line sooner.

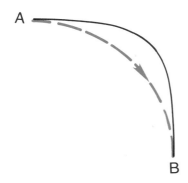

The common mistake of cutting into the circle during the last quarter of the circle is shown below:

In this case the skater started "across" to the Center too soon. Instead, she should have skated "down" the side line longer (until reaching the eighth) before starting to aim across to the Center.

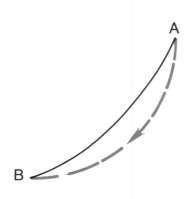

Below you see various mistakes on circles. See if you can tell which direction was maintained too long and which direction needed to be added in sooner. The correct circle is shown by a dotted red line and the skated circle is shown by a solid black line.

1. This skater went ___*accross the center*___ too soon

and needed to go ___*out*___ longer.

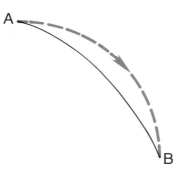

2. This skater aimed ___*Up the center*___ too soon

and needed to direct herself ___*out*___ longer.

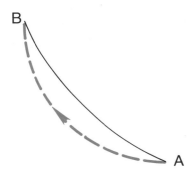

3. This skater directed the blade ___*Up the Side line*___

too long and needed to skate ___*in*___ sooner.

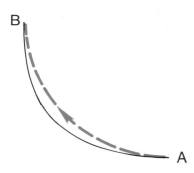

1. Down, Right Across   2. Up, Left Across   3. Left Across, Up

Grade Sheet

This is a grade sheet for you to pull out and take to your patch. Ask your coach for permission to skate your first figure with no marks on the ice and then to judge the figure according to the concepts on this sheet. Show your coach the results you recorded and see how you are progressing on the ice. The concepts on this page are derived from the first four lessons.

Circle Size

a) Walk the length and width of your first circle and record the number of steps.

Length   x   Width

b) Walk the length and width of your second circle and record the number of steps.

Length   x   Width

c) Walk the length and width of your third circle (on a serpentine) and record the number of steps.

Length   x   Width

Side Line Up:

Stand at each side of your figure. Look to see if the circles are in line with each other and parallel to the patch line.

a) Is the right side lined up?   yes   no   *(circle one)*
b) Is the left side lined up?   yes   no   *(circle one)*

Shape of Each Quarter Circle

Make a mark at the 1st quarter, the half and the 3rd quarter. Examine each quarter circle and judge to see if it is 1) Round or 2) Too much: left across   up   down   right across. Circle one for each quarter.

Circle 1

1st quarter is   round   or too much: left across   up   down   right across
2nd quarter is   round   or too much: left across   up   down   right across
3rd quarter is   round   or too much: left across   up   down   right across
4th quarter is   round   or too much: left across   up   down   right across

Circle 2

1st quarter is   round   or too much: left across   up   down   right across
2nd quarter is   round   or too much: left across   up   down   right across
3rd quarter is   round   or too much: left across   up   down   right across
4th quarter is   round   or too much: left across   up   down   right across

1. Into how many pieces does the long axis divide the circle? __two__

Are they the same size? __yes__

2. Into how many pieces do the hidden short axis lines cut the circle? __four__

(with the long axis drawn also)

3. The widest points of the circle are called?

__quarters__

4. When you skate through the 1st quarter of the circle are you skating parallel to or perpendicular to the side boards of the rink? __perpendicular__

5. Is a short axis line *parallel* or *perpendicular* to the long axis?

(circle one)

6. What does it mean to line up the sides of the figure? __to skate the quarters so they lay on a line parallel to the long axis__

7. What parts of the circle are you skating through when you are parallel to the sideboards of the rink? __The half and the center__

8. What are the four directions that you face while skating a circle?

__Center__   __1st quarter__   __2d quarter__   __3d quarter__

9. The direction at the eighth is __C__ to the sides of the square.
   a) parallel   b) perpendicular   c) diagonal   d) vertical

turn page for answers

31

In the 1920's the number of figures skated in competition was reduced to six. Figures then totalled 60% of the final score. This remained true until Trixie Schuba won the 1972 Olympics: Trixie placed 9th in free skating but won the competition because she was soo far ahead in figures. After that the rules were changed so that only three figures were skated and a short program was added.

Peggy Fleming USA. 1968 Olympic and World Champion
photo by American Broadcasting Corporation, Inc.

Karen Magnussen CAN. 1973 World Champion
1972 Olympic Silver Medalist
photo courtesy Gloria Magnussen

QUIZ ANSWERS
LESSONS 3 & 4

1. two, yes
2. four
3. quarters
4. perpendicular to

5. perpendicular to
6. to skate the quarters of each circle so they rest on a line parallel to the long axis
7. the half and the Center
8. left across, up, right across, down
9. c.) diagonal

Now that you've practiced your circles, let's see if you can draw just one quarter of each circle at a time. Below, the circles of a forward outside eight have been broken apart into four equal parts or arcs. Trace each of these quarter arcs 10 times in the direction indicated. Starting with #1RFO continue in the order skated: #2RFO, #3RFO and #4RFO. "RFO" stands for the **R**ight **F**orward **O**uter edge and "LFO" stands for the **L**eft **F**orward **O**uter edge. Continue by tracing #1LFO, #2LFO, #3LFO, and #4LFO 10 times before proceeding.

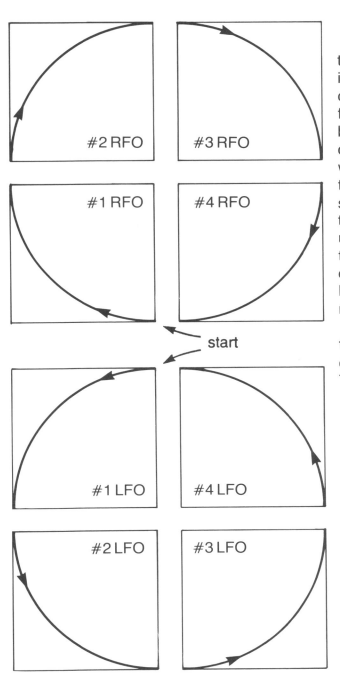

Why are you drawing quarter arcs of the circle? Well, when you stand on clean ice ready to skate a figure, the more clearly you can imagine the shape of the first quarter circle the better the circle will be. If the location of the quarter of the circle is wrong, then the length of the circle will be wrong: for example, if the circle is too narrow at the quarter, it is usually too short at the length. On the other hand, if the circle is too wide at the quarter it is usually too long at the half. Misjudging the location of the quarter can cause circles to have both incorrect width and length. As you can see this means you made two mistakes for the price of one!

Next, we are going to split the circle totally apart and individually look at each quarter arc. Why is this important to do? Turn the page and see.

Pretend you are on the ice about to skate a figure. Before starting the figure, imagine the curve to be skated and locate the exact spot for the quarter of the circle. Once in motion on the circle, continue to project the circle 5 or 6 feet (150-180 cms.) in front of your skating foot. Drawing quarter arcs will help you to plan the circular path ahead of your foot. Then, as your figures become more complex, you will be able to plan the path into and out of a turn or Change of Edge.

Below you will have three chances to draw each quarter arc of the right forward outside circle (RFO). Trace the example on the left 10 times starting with the #1RFO where indicated. Then, try to draw it on your own in the squares provided on the right.

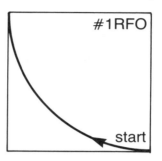 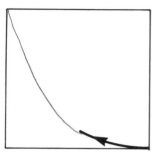 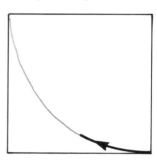 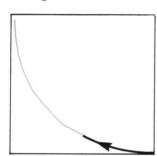

Good. Now trace quarter arc #2RFO 10 times before trying on your own in the squares on the right.

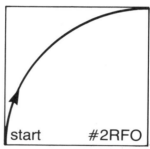 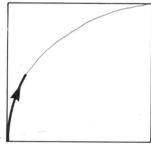 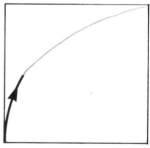 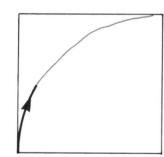

Follow the example for #3RFO 10 times. Then draw it on your own.

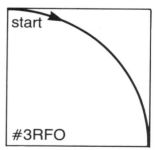 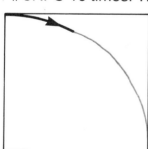 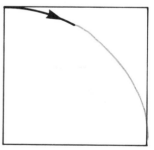 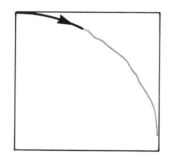

Trace #4RFO 10 times before drawing it in the squares provided.

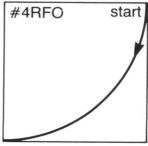 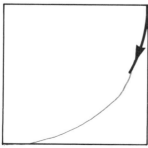 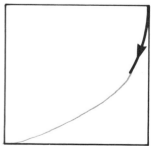 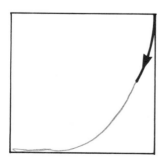

Each of these arcs curves in a clockwise direction.

Repeat the previous exercises for the right foot again. Start where the arrows indicate. This time you have no example. So in your mind, picture the curve you want to draw before putting it on paper.

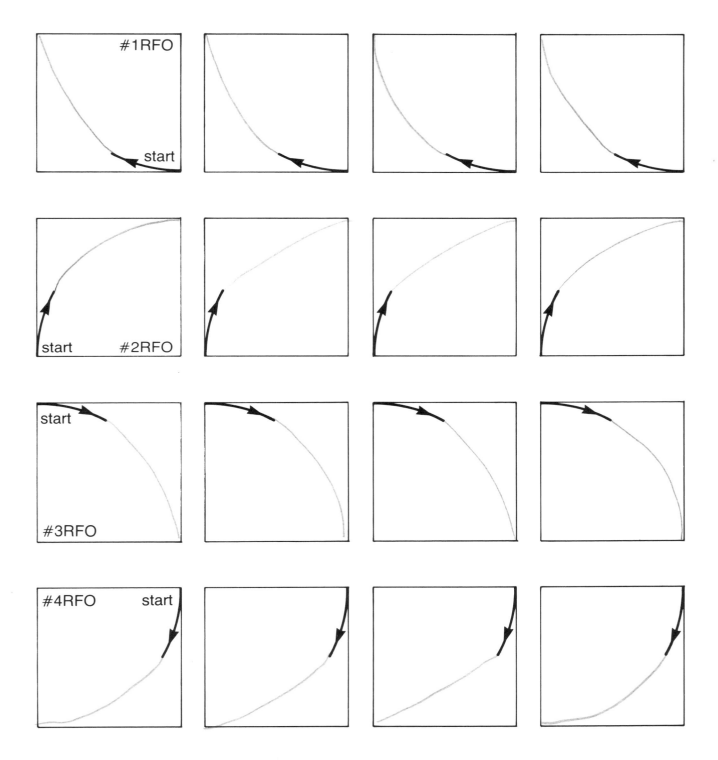

#1RFO

start

start   #2RFO

start

#3RFO

#4RFO   start

Do the same exercise going in the opposite direction, as if you were skating on your left forward outside (LFO) eight. Begin by tracing the example of #1LFO 10 times. Then practice drawing the arc in the remaining three squares. Start where the arrow indicates.

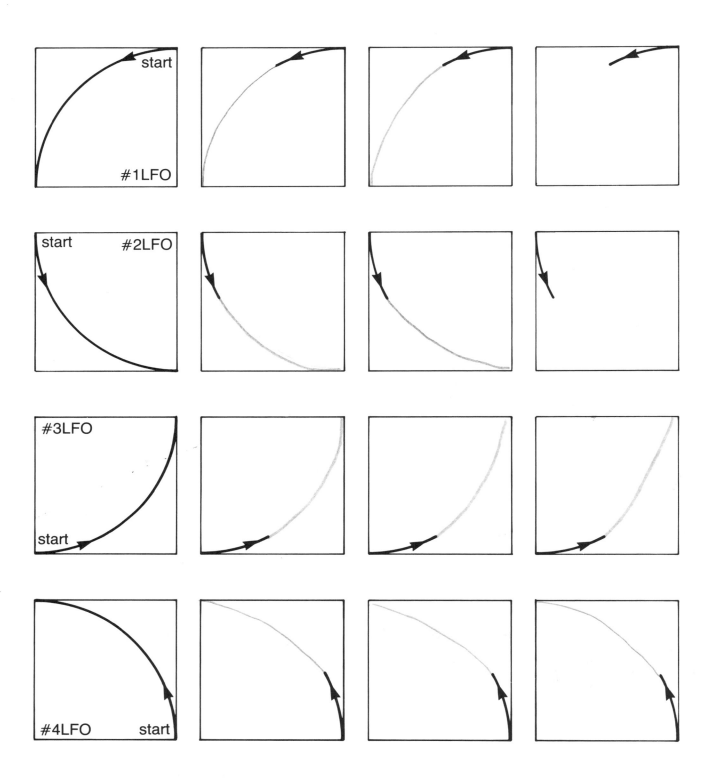

The four arcs you have just drawn are similar to the four quarter arcs of the right forward outside (RFO) eight. The only difference is that now the arcs are turning in a counterclockwise direction.

Going counterclockwise again (as if skating on your left foot) fill in the squares below with quarter arcs. Picture in your mind the path of the arc and then draw it. In each case start where the arrows indicate.

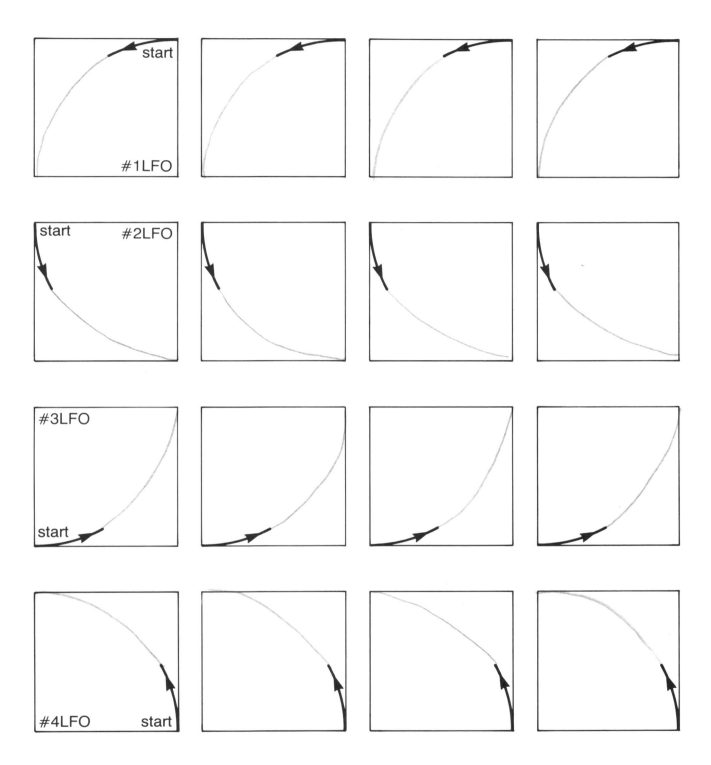

While you are skating a figure, it is important to project at least one quarter of the circle ahead of your skating foot. This way you will be able to project where turns and changes belong as you skate the figure.

This page has been provided for you to practice any quarter arcs that you may want to practice.

WORDS OF CAUTION

When skating circles on the ice, **DO NOT STEER YOUR FOOT** onto the curve you visualize. Steering is a major problem on the ice because it means you are forcing your foot to curve one way or another. When you steer your foot, you are restricting the natural flow and glide of the blade.

The goal of these exercises is to refine the image of the arc in your mind. *Your mental image is a guideline for circles, it doesn't create the circle.* Once you push off, just **ALLOW** your foot to skate the circle. Let your foot glide freely and it will automatically skate the circle you imagine.

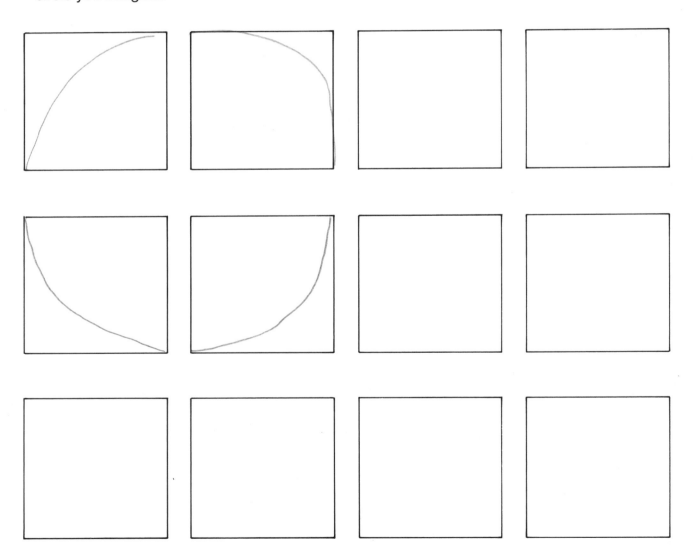

Again, the squares are arranged as if a full circle were being skated, but one arc at a time. Trace the example below as if you were skating your forward outside eight. Draw around. #1RFO, #2RFO, #3RFO, #4RFO and #1LFO, #2LFO, #3LFO, #4LFO. Repeat this sequence 10 times. Then on the right side of the page try drawing each circle on your own.

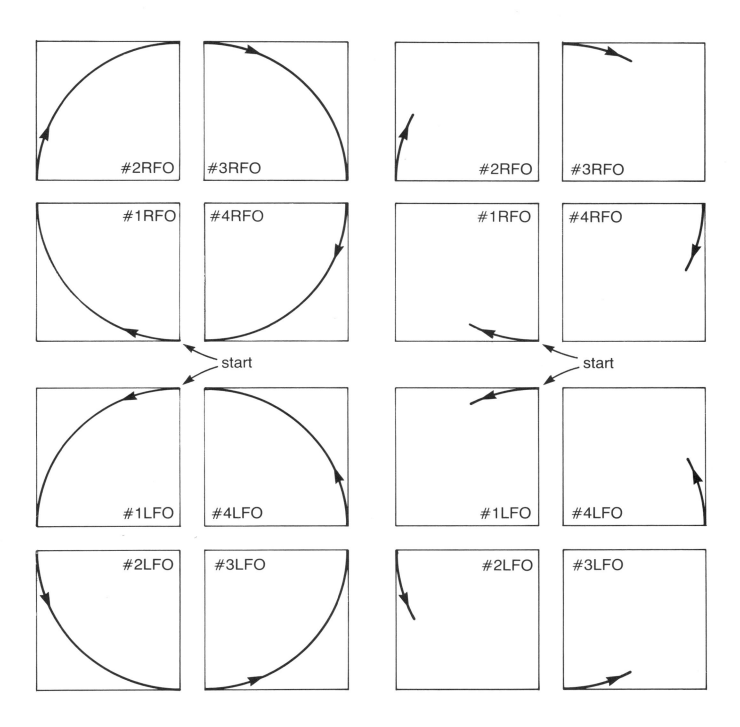

#2RFO

#3RFO

#1RFO

#4RFO

start

#1LFO

#4LFO

#2LFO

#3LFO

#2RFO

#3RFO

#1RFO

#4RFO

start

#1LFO

#4LFO

#2LFO

#3LFO

39

An example below is provided for a forward inner eight beginning in a counterclockwise direction. Draw each arc in the order indicated: #1RFI, #2RFI, #3RFI, #4RFI changing to #1LFI, #2LFI, #3LFI, #4LFI. Repeat this sequence 10 times before drawing them freehand on the right side of the page. Remember that you are learning to project the path of the quarter circle ahead of your foot.

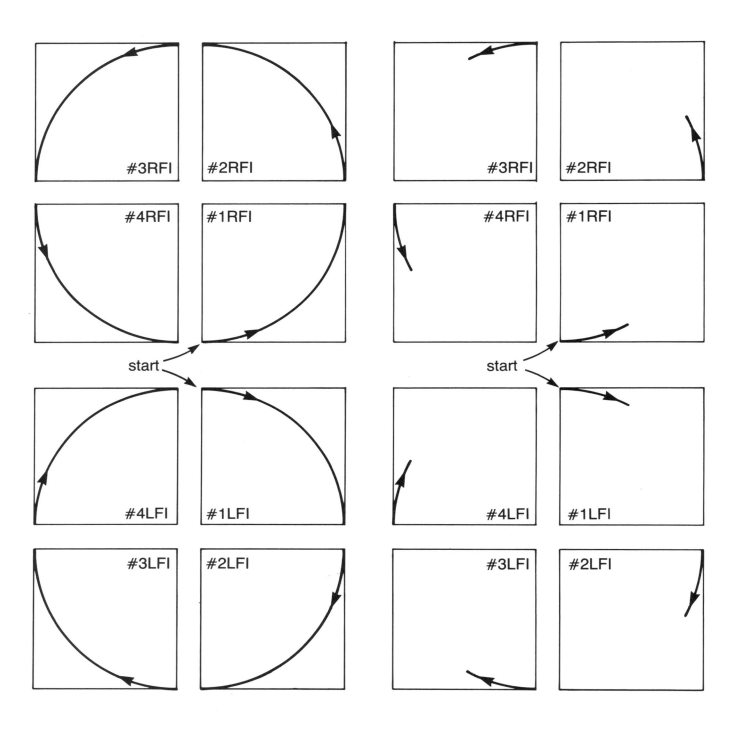

Repeat this exercise on the next two pages.

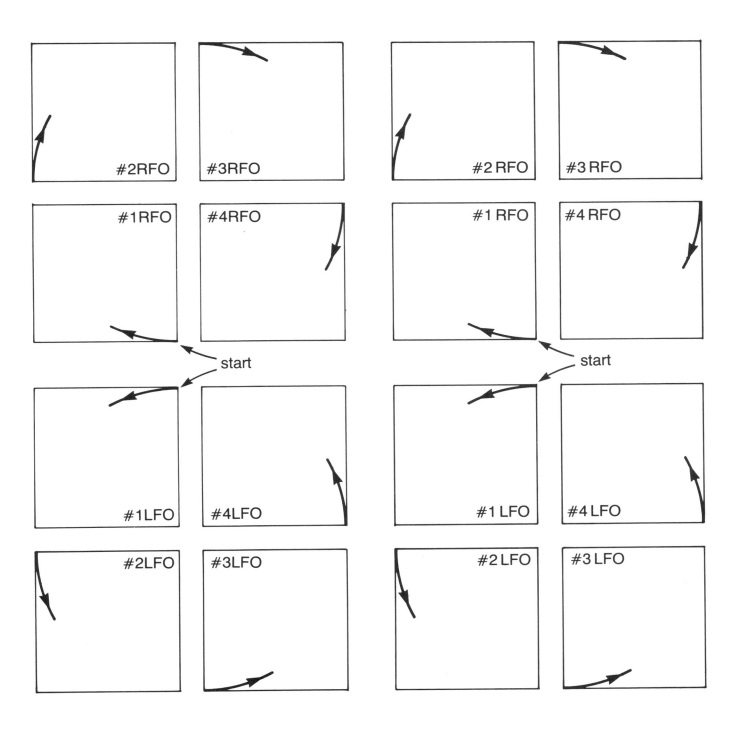

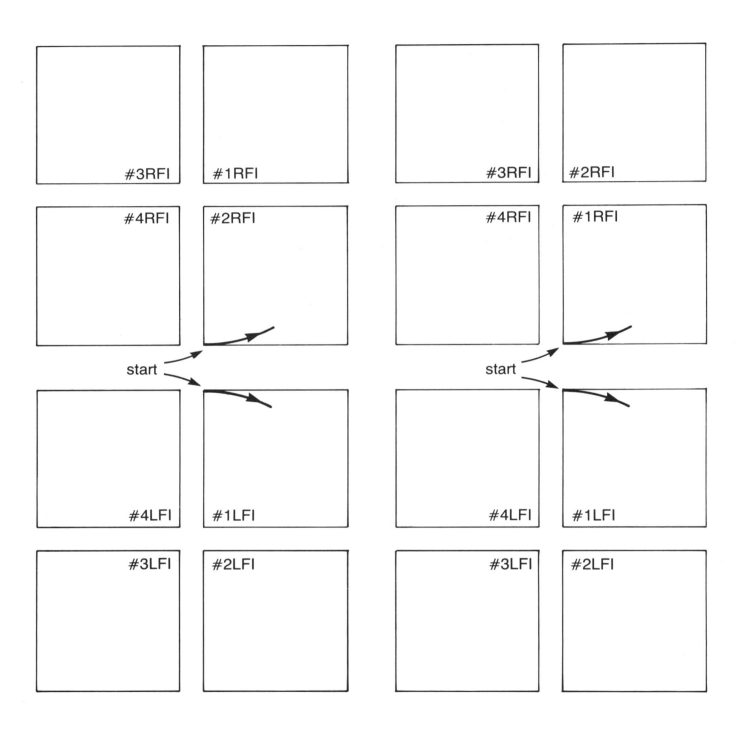

#3RFI #1RFI #3RFI #2RFI

#4RFI #2RFI #4RFI #1RFI

start start

#4LFI #1LFI #4LFI #1LFI

#3LFI #2LFI #3LFI #2LFI

Below, the smaller squares are glued back together to make one large square for a full circle. Start where indicated and in one smooth motion draw a circle in each square without lifting you pencil. Move your arm in a smooth, even, and relaxed motion, allowing your pencil to glide freely. Whether you are aware of this or not, you are judging where the path is going to go before your pencil ever gets there.

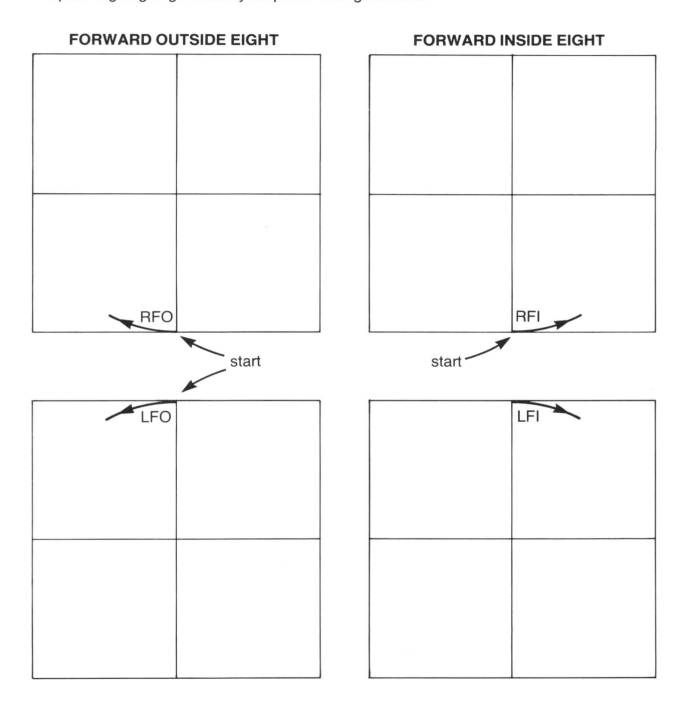

FORWARD OUTSIDE EIGHT

FORWARD INSIDE EIGHT

Skating is always on curved pathways. Each time you change feet, you either stay on the same curve (as in crossovers) or you change circles. When changing feet in a figure eight, do you change circles or stay on the same circle? Since you change circles when changing feet on a figure eight, we call it a two-lobe figure. A **LOBE** is a full circle, a curve, an arc, or any part of a circle. A serpentine is then called a three-lobe figure because it consists of three circles or lobes.

On this page the squares are joined together so you can draw a figure eight. Draw each circle as you would skate it with the pushes included. Start one eight clockwise and the other counterclockwise.

FORWARD OUTSIDE EIGHT

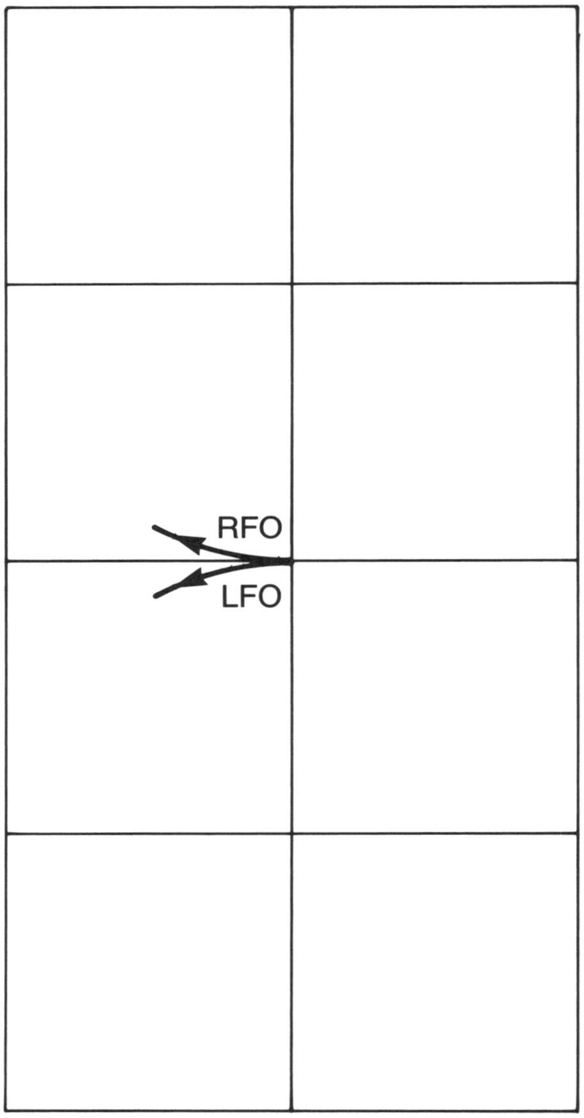

RFO

LFO

FORWARD INSIDE EIGHT

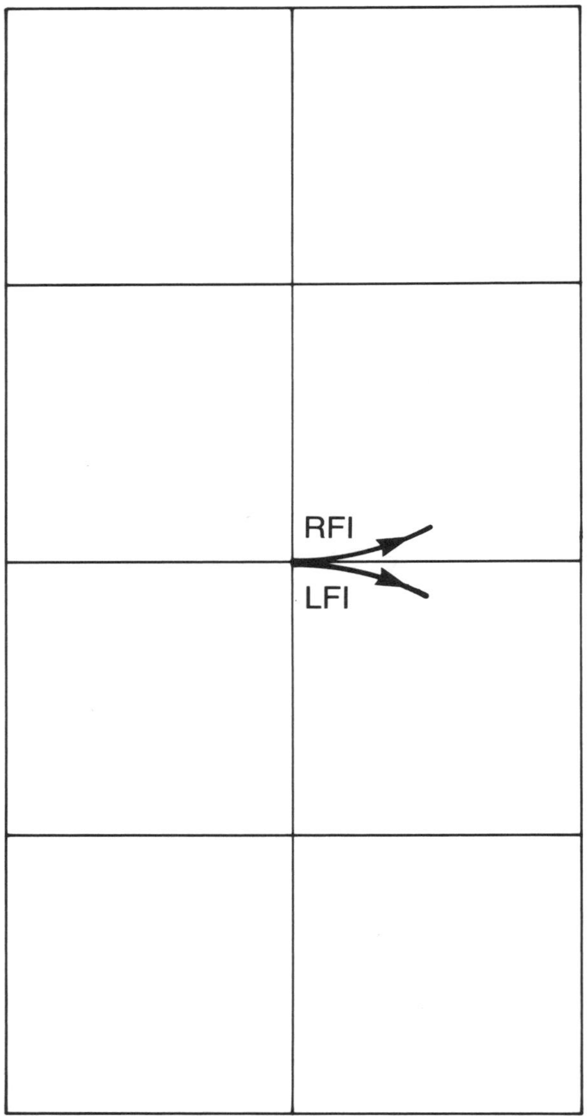

RFI

LFI

The circles or lobes you skate can be any size. A large lobe might fill half the rink and include back crossovers, a waltz jump, and left forward outside threes. On the other hand, a back inside pivot fits on a very tiny lobe. In figures your circles or lobes should be about three times your height, or usually 15 to 18 feet (about 6 meters) in diameter. A loop circle needs to measure equal to your height or about 55 to 65 inches (125-150 cms.) in diameter. A fun exercise might be to draw your free style program. See how many lobes it has and note whether or not the program has variation in lobe sizes and directions.

LESSON 6

Centers

This lesson focuses on the drawing of the Center, the change of foot and the pushes. Why are Centers important? High quality figures have neat, precise Centers. While skating on the circle your margin of error can be as much as 4 to 5 inches (9-11 cms.), but your margin of error at the Center can only be ½ to 1 inch (1½ to 2½ cms.).

We will look at the four basic figure eights and the differences among their pushes. All figures have a Center that combines the parts of these basic eight Centers.

The Center is divided into two parts: 1) the **PUSH** sometimes called the **THRUST** and 2) the **STEPDOWN** or **STRIKE** onto the new skating foot.
Look at the picture of the Forward Outside Eight Center below:

FORWARD OUTSIDE EIGHT CENTER

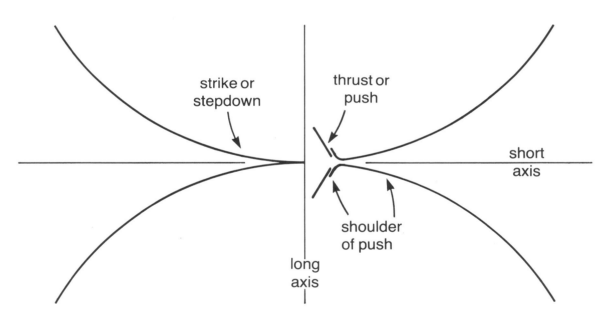

Notice the change of edge on the forward outside push or thrust. Most pushes occur from an inside edge. However, since you are skating on an outside edge upon entering the Center, you must change edge to push. It's important that this change of edge occur after your skate has turned off the circle into the push. Precision at the Centers is crucial for the skating of high quality figures. Pay attention to the following details.

Notice where the pushes are placed in relation to the long axis and to each other. On the ice, the pushes will be one blade length away from the long axis. Also note the angle of the pushes to the short axis. The gap between the **SHOULDERS** of the push should be no more than 1 inch (2½ cms.) on the ice. The shoulder of the push consists of the turn of the push and the circle just before it. See the illustration.

The Forward Inside Eight Center is drawn below. Notice how this Center appears different from the Forward Outside Eight Center. Inside pushes always cross each other and the short axis while they glide into the next skating circle.

FORWARD INSIDE EIGHT CENTER

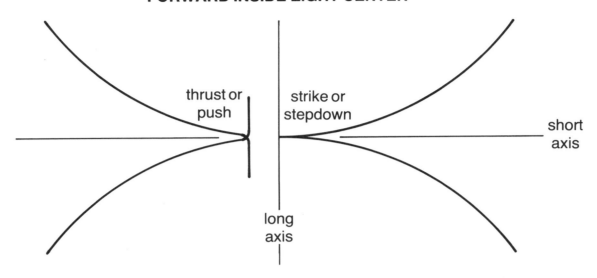

The secret to skating good inside Centers is to turn your foot onto the push immediately after crossing the tracings. The point where the pushes cross must be on the short axis itself about 10 inches (or 23cms.) from the long axis.

In order to be opposite each other, all the pushes must cross the short axis at precisely the same point. We call this point where the pushes turn and cross on the short axis the **POINT OF PIVOT** (P.O.P.). Pretend there is a bubble on the short axis exactly 10 inches (23cms.) from the long axis. When skating the Center, let the ball of your foot P.O.P. the bubble. Then pivot or turn your foot to the side for the push. As long as each push aims for the same Point of Pivot, they should all be opposite each other and well traced.

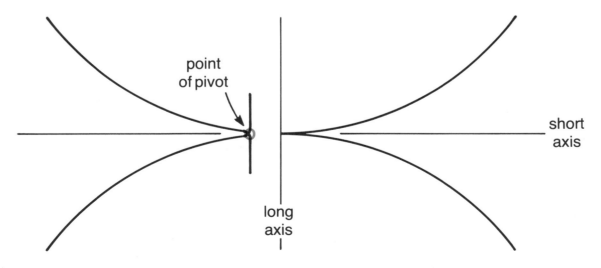

The Point of Pivot is always at the bottom of the first push and in line with the first strike or step down. The Point of Pivot and the first strike need to be on the same short axis.

Learn to stand back and examine a figure that you have skated just as the judges will stand back and look at it.

When judges examine your figure, they stop and pay careful attention to your Center. Therefore, *you* need to pay attention to your Center.

There are four aspects to good Centers:

1) Symmetry

The circles into and out of the Center are a mirror image of each other (symmetrical)* in two ways. See picture below.

2) Pushes

The pushes are traced and located one blade length from the long axis. Try to make your pushes close enough to each other to be covered by three of your fingers. As you improve you can aim to skate "two finger" pushes.

3) Edges

The edges on the circle into the push are clean with no flats on inner pushes. The outside edge changes at the correct location on outer pushes (after your foot has turned into the push).

4) Stepdowns

The stepdowns or strikes are clean (on the proper edge) with no scuffs or scrapes. They must be the correct shape so you start on a true circle.

*SYMMETRICAL means both halves of an image are identical in size, shape and location. Your body is symmetrical because the right half is identical to the left half of your body. On each side you have one arm, one leg, one eye, one ear - each the same size and shape and situated in the same place as on the other side.

A Center has a symmetrical, mirror image when viewed from two different locations. Look at pictures # 1 and # 2.

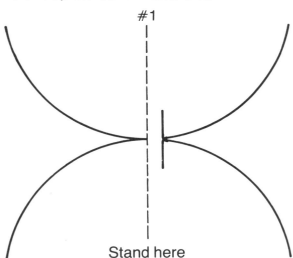

#1

Stand here

If you divide the picture in half along the dotted line, does the right half look like the left half? (except for the pushes)

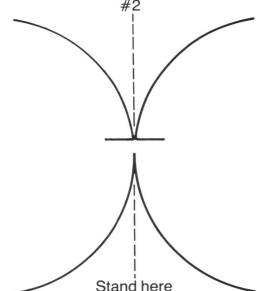

#2

Stand here

If you divide this picture in half along the dotted line, does the right half look like a reflection of the left half?

It is always important for you to stand at these two spots and examine your Center to see if indeed it is symmetrical from both these viewpoints. If your answer is yes to both questions above, then your Center is truly symmetrical.

Centers are the part of the figure where you change lobes. On a good figure each lobe is the same size and shape. It is tricky to push, change feet, and change lobes without distorting the curve or shape of the circle. However, if you can skate through the Center and maintain the symmetry of the circles (that is maintain the same size and shape), then you will have a good Center. The exercises on the following pages are designed to help you achieve this goal.

On this page you are provided with two Centers. Trace each one by drawing from A to B and then from C to D. Trace 10 times over each entry/exit from the Center. Feel how one circle continues into the next. Notice the symmetry of the shoulders of the pushes, the pushes, and the strikes.

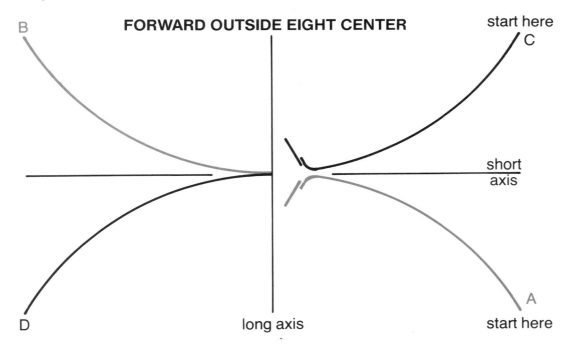

FORWARD OUTSIDE EIGHT CENTER

start here
C

B

short
axis

D   long axis   A
                              start here

Be precise with your pencil. Carefully trace the push and then position your pencil precisely on the short axis to begin the circle out of the Center. Remember the blade of your skate can be as precise on the ice as the pencil in your hand.

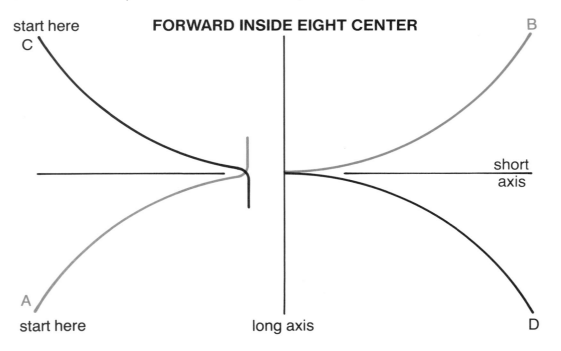

start here
C

FORWARD INSIDE EIGHT CENTER

B

short
axis

A
start here   long axis   D

Now draw your own Forward Outside Eight Center: Start at point A

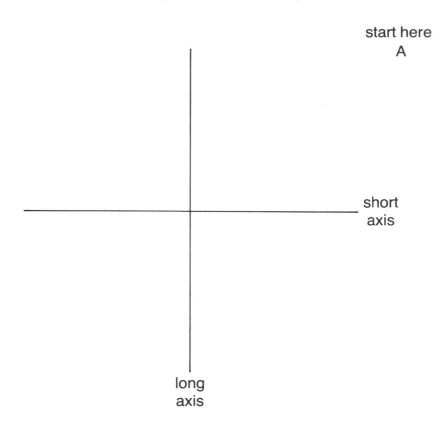

start here
A

short
axis

long
axis

Now draw your own Forward Inside Eight Center: Start at point A and aim for the Point of Pivot (P.O.P.). Make sure that your pushes cross each other and the short axis at the Point of Pivot.

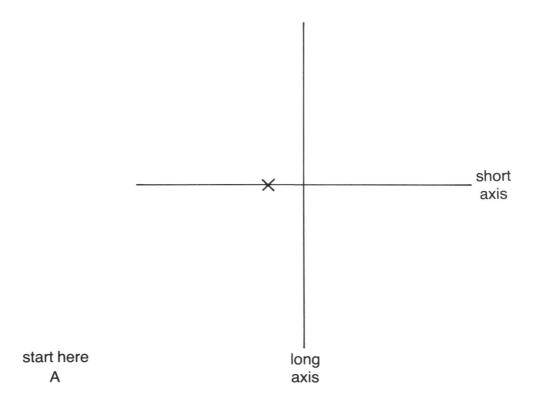

short
axis

start here
A

long
axis

A Back Outside Eight Center is similar to the Forward Outside Eight Center only the pushes are longer and shaped differently. The pushing foot should leave the ice before crossing the long axis. Judges take points off for pushes that **Trail** too long on the ice because it means you are really balancing on two feet (which is cheating). On outside eights the Point of Pivot is in the gap between the pushes.

BACK OUTSIDE EIGHT CENTER

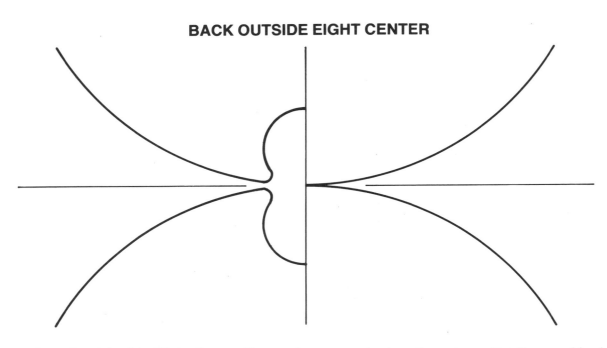

On a Back Inside Eight Center the pushes cross just as they do on the Forward Inside Eight. It is especially tricky to keep the edge clean while turning it for the push. On inside eights the Point of Pivot should be at the spot where the pushes cross. If you were skating a back inside push, you should aim the heel of your blade through the Point of Pivot. When the ball of your foot is on the Point of Pivot, turn your heel into the push. If you do this, your pushes will always be opposite each other.

BACK INSIDE EIGHT CENTER

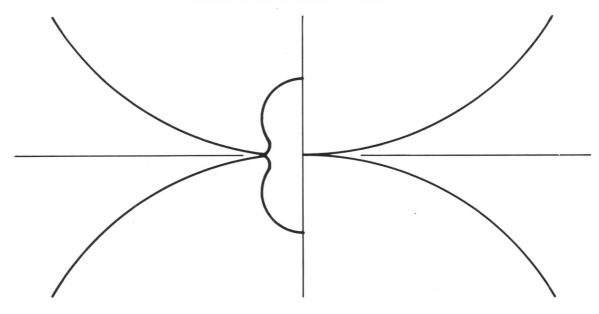

Here are two Centers for your practice. Trace each one 10 times by following one edge from point A to point B and then point C to D.

BACK OUTSIDE EIGHT CENTER

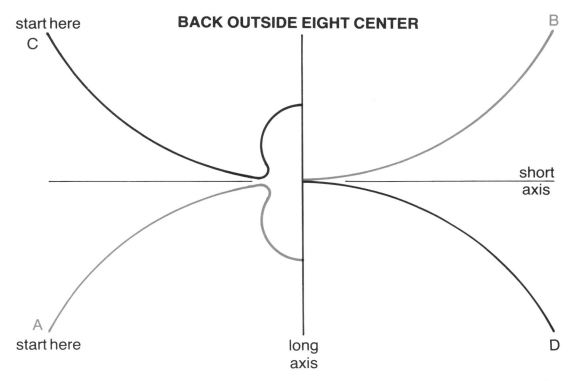

Go slowly enough to be precise at your Centers while maintaining an even flow. One way to test your symmetry is to pick a spot on the short axis like "E" below. Measure the distance from spot "E" to the curve on each side of the short axis. If the curves are symmetrical, the distance will be the same on each side. You should be able to pick any spot on the short axis of any figure and do this test. If the curves are **NOT** symmetrical, the distance on one side will be larger than the distance to the curve on the other side.

BACK INSIDE EIGHT CENTER

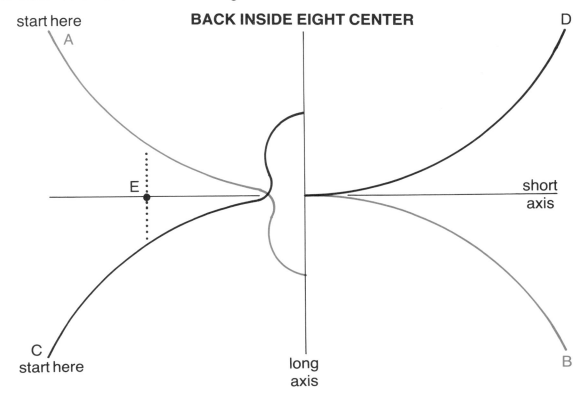

Now draw your own Back Outside Eight Center on the axis provided. Decide where the Point of Pivot should be before you begin and aim for that spot when drawing the Center. Make the pushes and the shoulders of the pushes symmetrical (the same size and shape). Feel how one circle continues into the next circle.

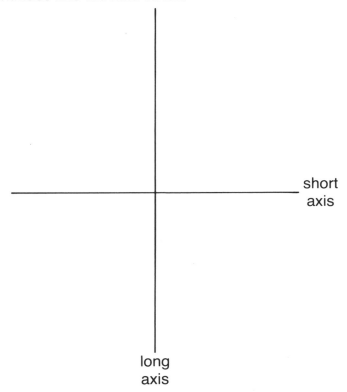

short
axis

long
axis

Draw your own Back Inside Eight Center on the axis provided. The Point of Pivot is at the botttom of the first push off. Compare your drawing to the pictures on the previous page. Each push should be the same shape and length as the other one.

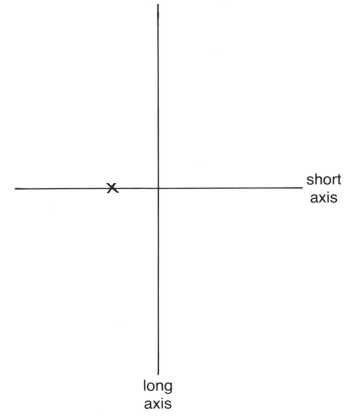

short
axis

long
axis

Pretend you are standing on clean ice about to skate a figure. After you push off, the following marks are left on the ice.

You have just created your short axis and your long axis just by pushing off. Use your ruler to draw in the short and long axis on the 3 examples above. The short axis connects the top of the push and the bottom of the stepdown. It is determined by the top of the push and must run perpendicular to the long axis. The long axis is also determined by the push and strike. The long axis is one blade length from the push and the strike should begin at that point.

Each time you skate through the Center continue to use the same short axis. Any turns or Changes of Edge must lie on the same long axis as that first Center. Below are some examples of mistakes where the short axis has been moved from the original location as the skater passed through the Center the second time.

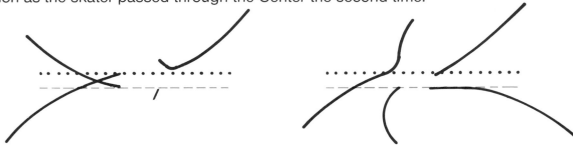

Another mistake is to have the first push on one short axis and the initial stepdown on a different axis as shown:

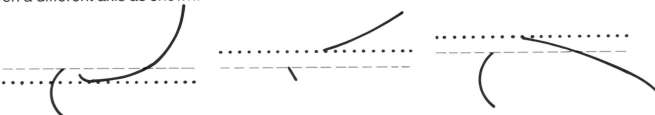

An **OPEN** Center means that you haven't skated your pushes close enough to each other. They should almost touch. This is a major mistake and looks like:

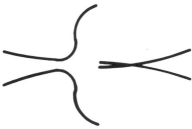

On the ice, **TOE PUSHES** (pushing from your toe pick) are a common error on forward pushes. If your pushing foot doesn't turn to the side before thrusting from the toe pick, this is the worst type of toe push. This toe push is graded an "F" or lower. However, if your pushing foot turns to the side first before pressing from the toe pick, the error is not as serious. This type of toe push is graded as a "C" or average. To prevent this error altogether, always turn your foot into the push and keep your heel down when thrusting.

Some of the common mistakes that occur at Centers are listed below. If you skated a perfect Center it would receive a grade "A". Any mistakes bring your grade down depending upon how serious the mistake is and how many mistakes you combine. Usually one mistake creates another, so mistakes travel in teams of two, three or four. Examine the pictures below to see how certain mistakes are graded. Then look at your patch and grade yourself.

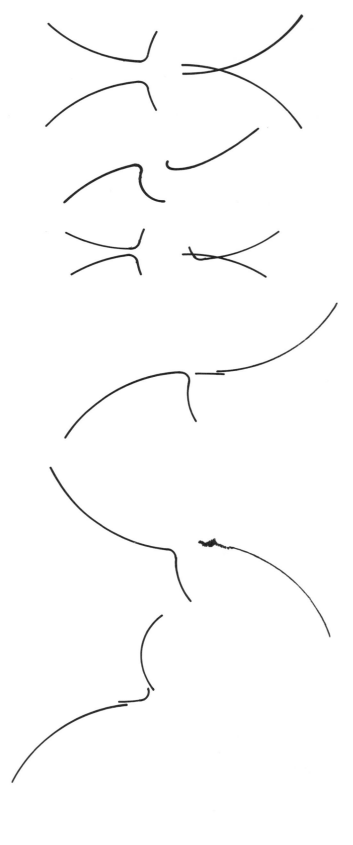

"B" 1) Stepdowns that cross each other are minor mistakes as long as they only cross a little bit. The more they cross the more points a judge deducts from your score.

"C" 2) The Back Outside stepdown **HOOKS** or curls before it turns onto the circle.

"D"   Often the hook crosses the other stepdown making the mistake more serious.

"D" 3) Change of edge on a stepdown: this mistake usually occurs on a back outside strike where your foot touches the ice on an inside edge for several inches before it changes to a back outside edge.

"D" 4) A scrape or skid on a stepdown usually occurs on a back inside strike. It is called a **SLITCHED** stepdown. This is made by the ball of your foot sliding across the ice before completely transferring your weight onto the new skating foot.

"D" 5) A change of edge before a forward inside or back inside push is a major mistake. With the circle on an inside edge **AND** the push on an inside edge, there is no reason for the edge to change at any point. In fact the entire figure is on an inside edge.

QUIZ
LESSONS
5 and 6

1. When a circle is too wide in the 1st quarter, then at the half it will probably be too

long   or   short   *(circle one)*.

2. How many figure eights have a change of edge on the pushes? _____
Name them: _____   _____

3. Which two figure eights have pushes that always cross at the Center?

_____   _____

4. What is another name for a push? _____

5. What is another name for a stepdown? _____

6. Where should inside pushes cross? Draw a Center with long axis, short axis and pushes and indicate where the pushes should cross. _____

7. When a judge examines your Center they look at four things. Name them.

_____   _____

_____   _____

8. Describe the worst kind of toe push.

_____

_____

turn page for answers   55

International Judges 1981 Worlds
photo by Fred Dean

Emi Watanabe JPN. 1979 World Bronze Medalist
photo by Fred Dean

QUIZ ANSWERS
LESSONS 5 & 6

1. long
2. two, Forward Outside Eights
   Backward Outside Eights
3. Forward Inside Eights
   Backward Inside Eights
4. thrust
5. strike
6. on the short axis one blade length from
the long axis on the ice

7. a: symmetry
   b: pushes
   c: stepdowns
   d: cleaness of edge
8. when your pushing foot doesn't turn to
the side before pressing from the toe pick

answers from page 8

LESSON 7

Half Circles and Serpentines

In lesson five, you divided the circle into four pieces and practiced drawing quarter arcs. Now, you are going to divide the circle into two pieces and practice drawing half circle arcs. Why? It is not enough to imagine only the 1st quarter of the circle. You have to locate the length in order to judge the half of the circle. Whether placing a three turn or skating a serpentine, a clear image of the distance from the Center to the first half of the circle is necessary.

The circles on this page have been broken into two equal pieces. Trace each half 10 times in the direction indicated beginning with #1RFO. Drawing half circles will help you to judge the location of the top of the circle. Before laying out a figure on clean ice, take a moment to judge the length of the circle. Pick a precise spot that marks the location of the half. Imagine the path of the circle which will lead to that spot. With your eyes on that spot, skate the circle. Practicing this technique on the following pages will help you perfect it on the ice.

FORWARD OUTSIDE EIGHT

#1 RFO

#2 RFO

start

#1 LFO

#2 LFO

Below you will have three chances to draw each half arc on your own. First, trace the example 10 times, starting where the arrow indicates. Then, draw each half arc in the rectangles on the right.

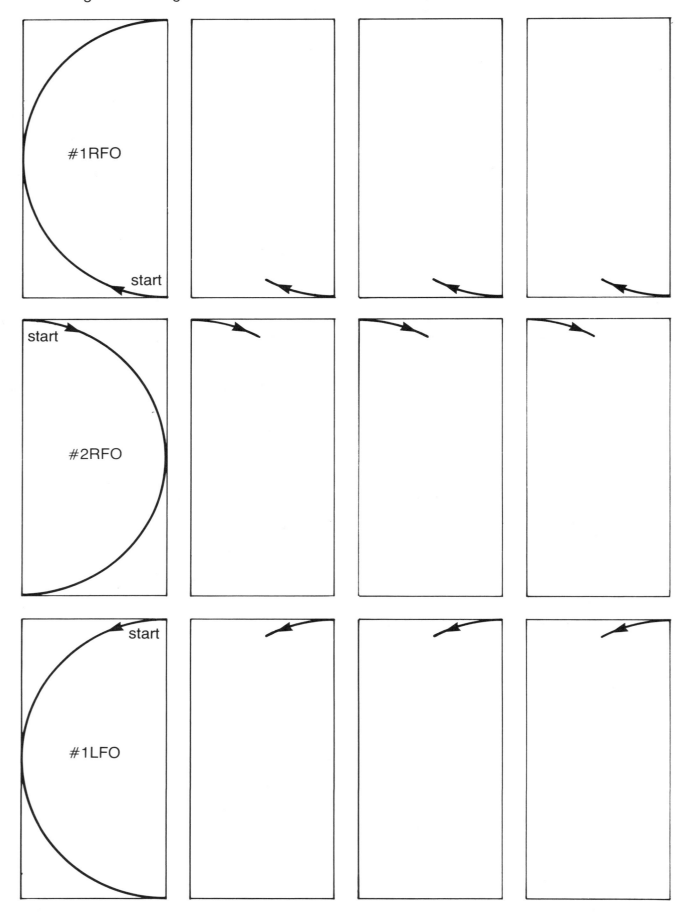

#1RFO   start

#2RFO   start

#1LFO   start

Continue on these pages to trace the example 10 times before drawing your own half arc. Try to judge where the quarter of the circle will touch the side of the rectangle; plan your circle so it touches the rectangle at that point.

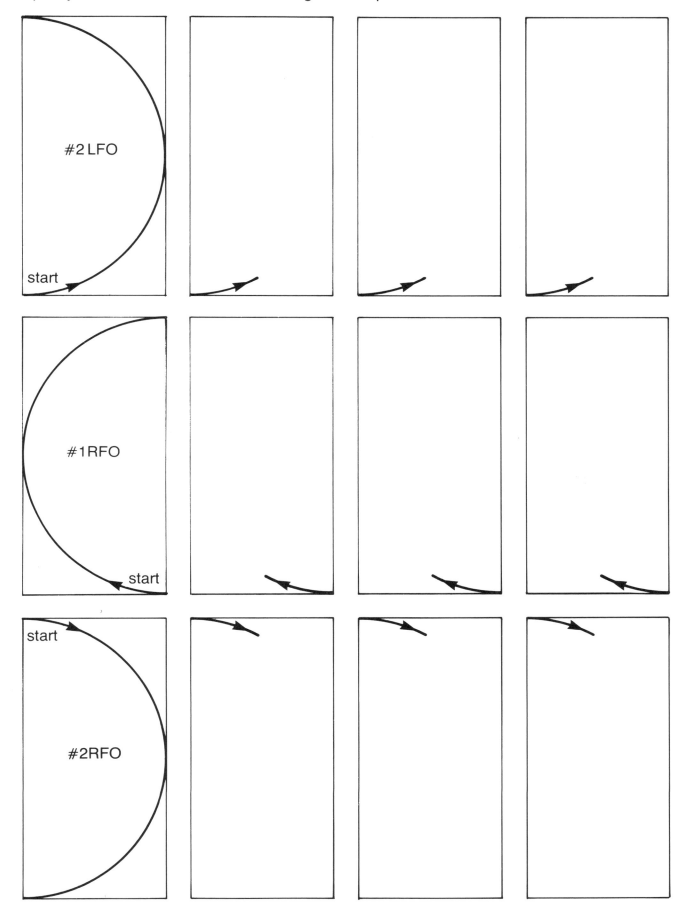

Trace and draw your half arc in one fluid motion. Use your whole arm to move your pencil with flow.

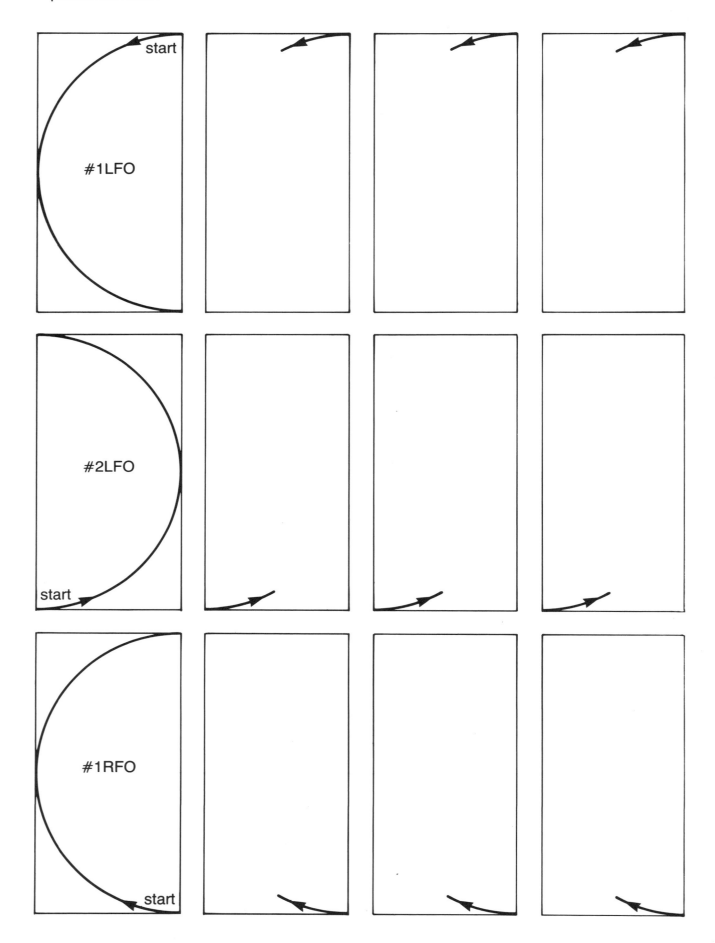

Now it's time to put the halves back together, but with a new twist: the two half circles are joined as if you were skating the first half of a serpentine. Trace each of these figures in the direction indicated 10 times. Each time you trace the figure, notice how the direction changes when you change circles. In other words when changing edge, you change circles. While skating the Change of Edge, it is important that you always CHANGE EDGE AND CHANGE CIRCLES at PRECISELY the SAME SPOT!

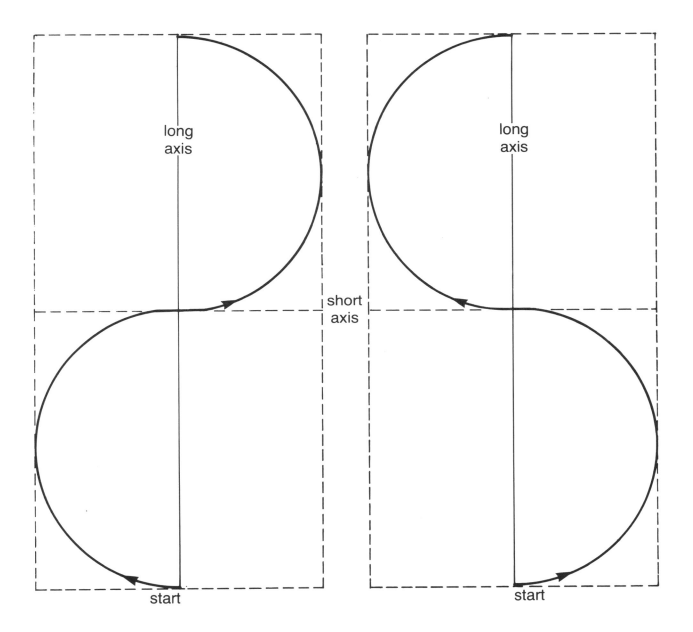

If you don't change circles when changing edge, you have skated what is called a **DOUBLE CHANGE**. This means you change edge first and change circle several inches later (picture A). This mistake could fail a figure. Sometimes a double change means that you tried to change circles twice (picture B).

Draw your own partial serpentines. Start where the arrow indicates. Check your drawing with a compass and trace the correct tracing. Judge the path of the half circle leading up to the change. Imagine where the quarter of the first circle will meet the side of the square before the change. After the change, plan where the circle will touch the side of the second square.

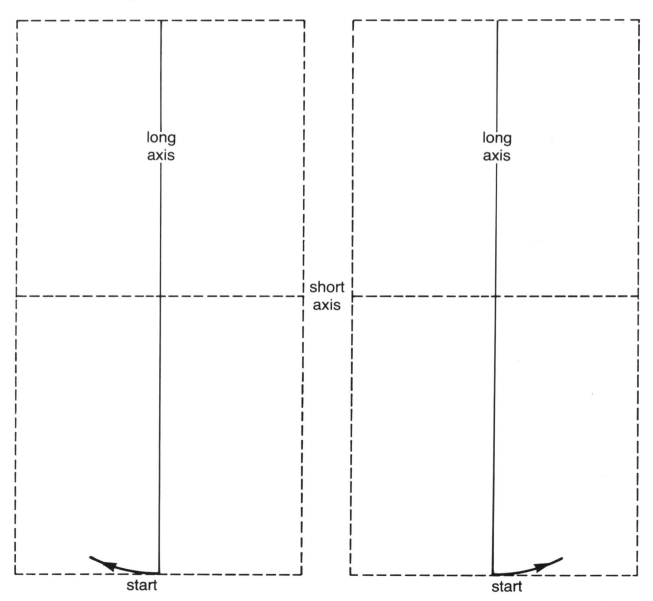

Continue to practice drawing your own partial serpentines. Start where the arrow indicates. Check your drawing with a compass and trace the correct tracing. When a judge examines a serpentine figure, he walks the length of each circle. If one circle is nine steps long, then all three circles need to be nine steps long. How wide should each circle be? (answer below).

A judge examines the change to locate the "flat" which marks the middle of the change. Then, he places a marker on the flat to indicate the long axis of the change. After a judge marks the skated long axis for both Centers, he stands back to see if both changes are lined up on the *same* long axis. If they aren't lined up within 4 inches (10 cms.) of each other, the judge considers it to be a major mistake. Major mistakes fail tests and lose competitions.

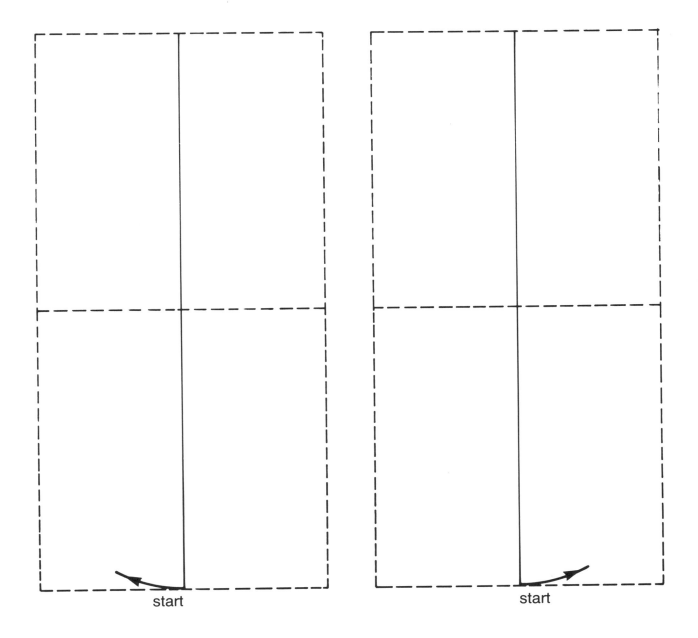

start   start

Answer: Nine

Imagine that you have just skated a Change of Edge on the ice (picture A). In skating the change, you have just defined the long axis and the short axis of that Center. The "flat" which occurs in the middle of the change results from the roll of the foot from one edge to the other. The middle of the "flat" is considered to be the long axis of that Center. The "flat" is really the Change of Edge itself. It is supposed to be perpendicular to the long axis and to define the short axis of the change. When gliding back into the Center for the inside push, look for the point where the change hits the short axis. See illustration B. This point is the Point of Pivot for the push. Draw the inside push to cross the change at that spot.

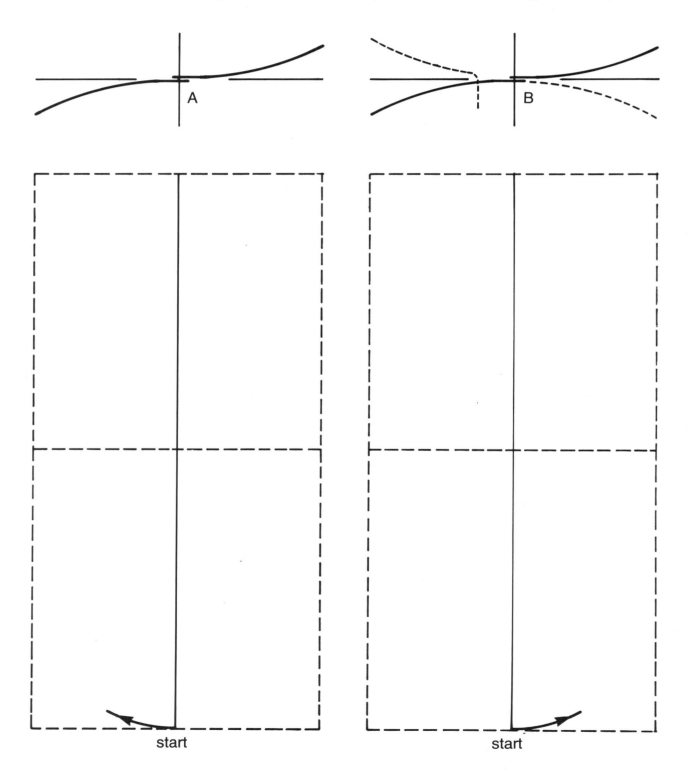

start   start

On this page we have drawn the second half of the serpentine in the opposite direction from before. Trace each one 10 times.

Notice how the Change of Edge follows the short axis for a brief time only. On the ice the Change of Edge follows the short axis for about two blade lengths. The Change of Edge should hit the short axis about one blade length *before* the long axis. It should leave the short axis about one blade length *after* the long axis. Short changes get higher points from judges.

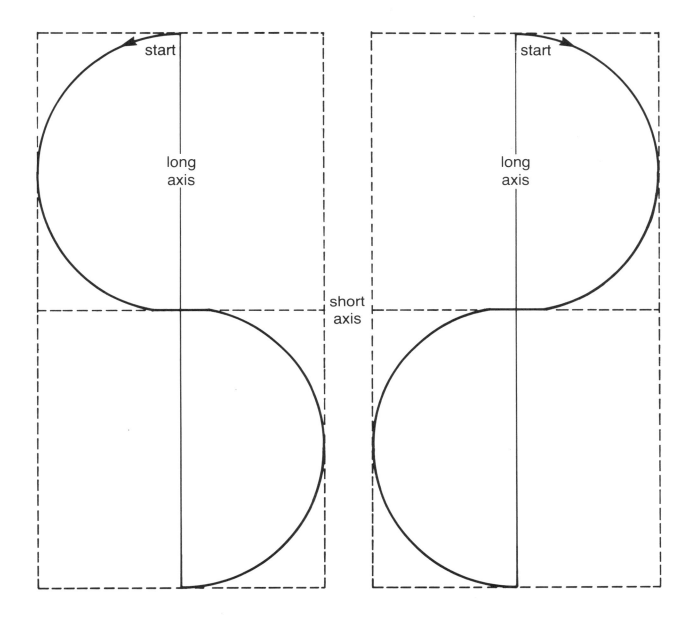

The first Change of Edge on a serpentine is skated on clean ice with the push and strike skated in later (see illustration A). However, the second change differs from the first one because the second change connects a push and strike (stepdown) that have already been skated (see illustration B). To make the second Change of Edge easier, it is a good idea to mark an "X" at the top of the push and an "X" at the beginning of the stepdown (see illustration C). Aim to connect these two points with your change of edge (see illustration D).

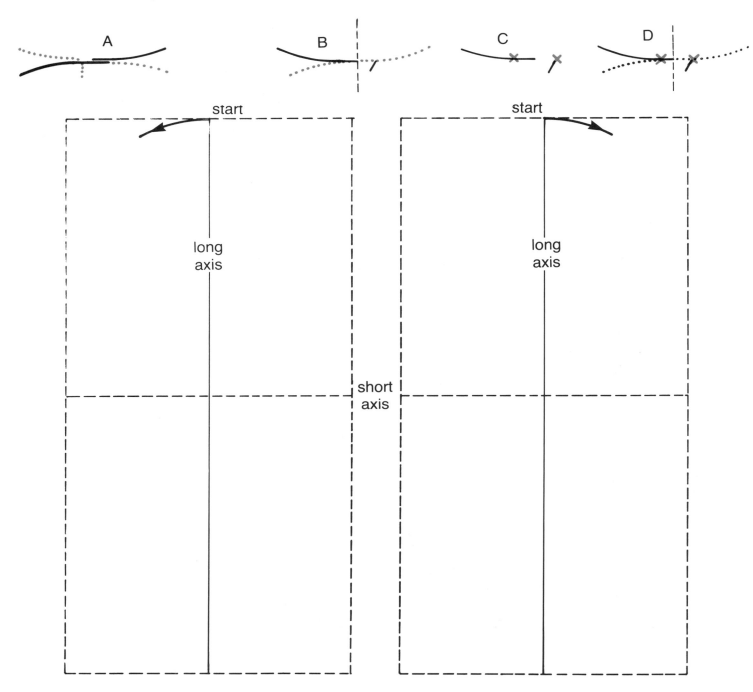

An **S'd change** is a common mistake when changing edge and circles. There are three common variations of an S'd change:

1. "S" or bulged *before* the long axis

2. "S" or bulged *after* the long axis

3. Double "S" or bulged *on both* sides of the long axis.

S'd changes are graded according to how much deviation there is from the true circle. Examples #1 and #2 might be graded as a "C" (average) if the S is small, only 1 or 2 inches (2-4 cms.). However, if the deviation from the circle is 5 or 6 inches (12-14 cms.), the change would be graded much lower. Example #3 is a more serious error because the tracing is far from the true circle on *both* sides of the change: this is considered to be a major error and would be graded as an "F" or fail.

Continue to draw your serpentines in the squares below. Start where the arrows indicate.

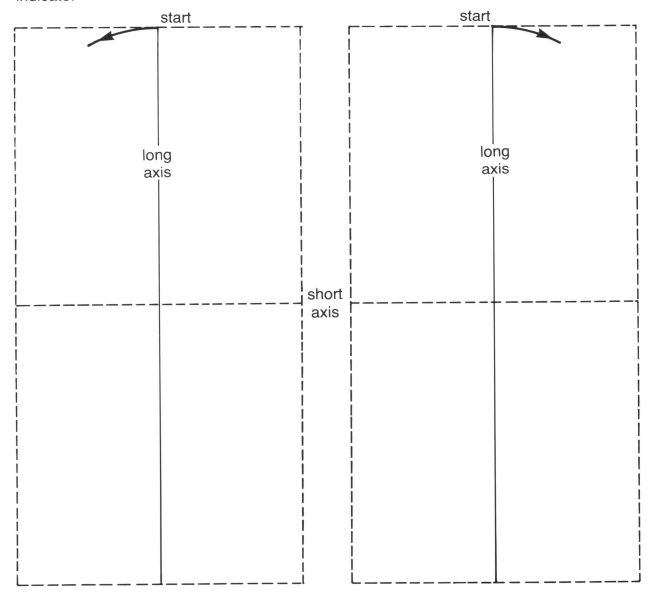

DIAGONAL CHANGES (like S'd changes) are graded by the amount of deviation from the true circle. On a Change of Edge that is diagonal the circle is flattened out or dented and appears as a straight line instead of a curve. Usually diagonal changes are graded hard by judges because they feel diagonal changes indicate little feel for the curve of the circle. Diagonal changes are almost always graded as a "D" or an "F" for fail. Sometimes a diagonal change is called an **OBLIQUE** change, because it runs at an angle to the short axis instead of on it. Just like S'd changes, there are three types of diagonal changes.

1. Diagonal or straight *before* the long axis.

2. Diagonal or dented *after* the long axis.

3. Diagonal on *both* sides of the long axis.

Continue to practice drawing your changes below. Check your drawing with a compass and correct if necessary.

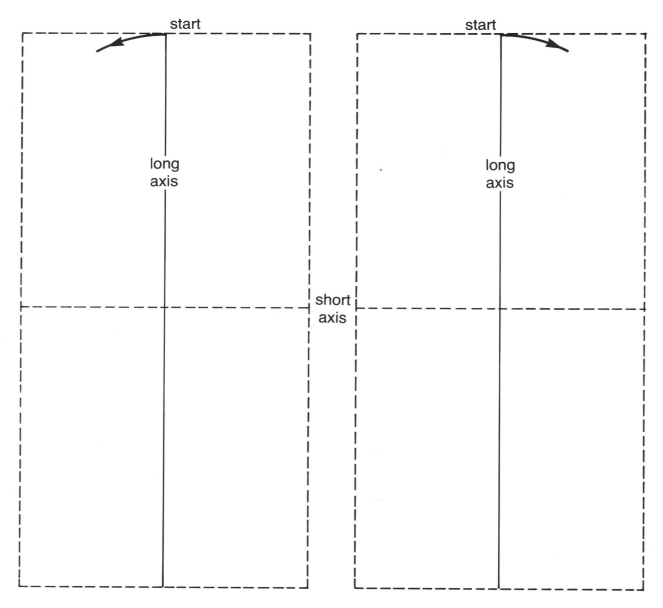

A *Three to Center* is drawn below because it is representative of any three turn figure (except double threes). The three is located at the half pointing directly towards the Center. The curves of the circle, three or four feet before and after the turn are called the **SHOULDERS of the TURN.** Any line drawn across the shoulders of the turn should run perpendicular to the long axis at the turn (see illustration). In order for the shoulders of the turn to be even, they should touch the short axis just before and after the turn.

Practice this figure 10 times on each circle provided. Draw the push as an extension of the circle. Shape the turns evenly on both sides and point them straight down the long axis towards the center of the circle.

Three turns are judged by their symmetry: judges look to see if both sides of the turn are the identical shape. Threes are also judged by their placement: judges stand at the top of the circle and imagine a line drawn from the three turn to the Center. If this line divides the circle into two equal halves, *and* if the turn is lined up with the long axis at the Center, then the judges consider the turn to be well placed.

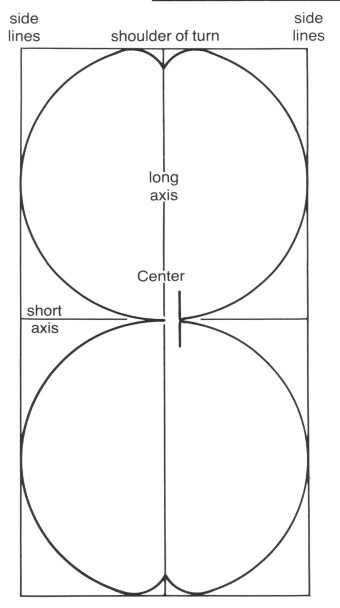

side lines

shoulder of turn

side lines

long axis

Center

short axis

On each of the following pages you are going to draw one figure from your current figure test. Two sets of squares have been provided on each page. In the set of squares on the left, a "scribed" circle has been drawn for you to trace a model of the first figure on your test. Filling in pushes and any turns, follow the model 10 times until you have the picture firmly drawn in your mind. In the remaining squares, draw three tracings of the same figure - only freehand. Correct your freehand figure with a compass and trace over the correction three more times. After completing this, move on to the next page.

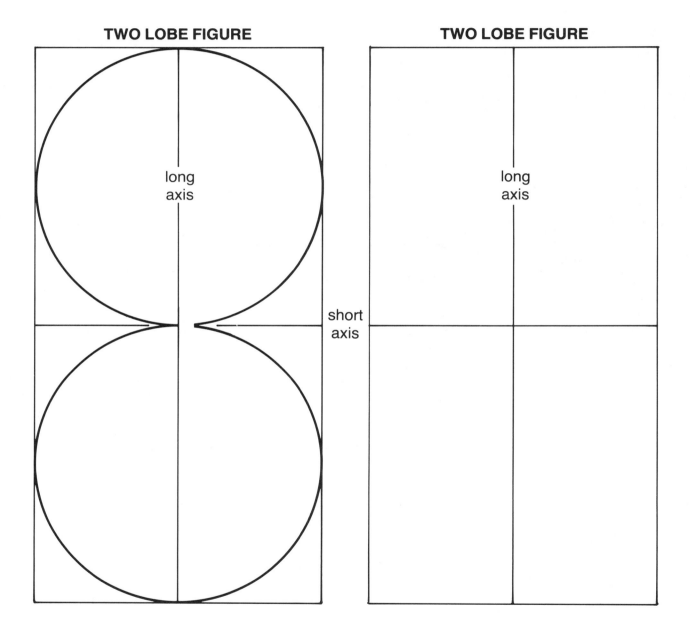

TWO LOBE FIGURE

long axis

short axis

TWO LOBE FIGURE

long axis

Draw the next figure of your test on the circle scribed on the left side of the page. After tracing it 10 times, draw the figure freehand on the right side of the page. Include all the pushes and turns as you would skate them. Correct your circles with a compass and trace the correction three more times. When you are satisfied with your circles, move on to the next page.

TWO LOBE FIGURE **TWO LOBE FIGURE**

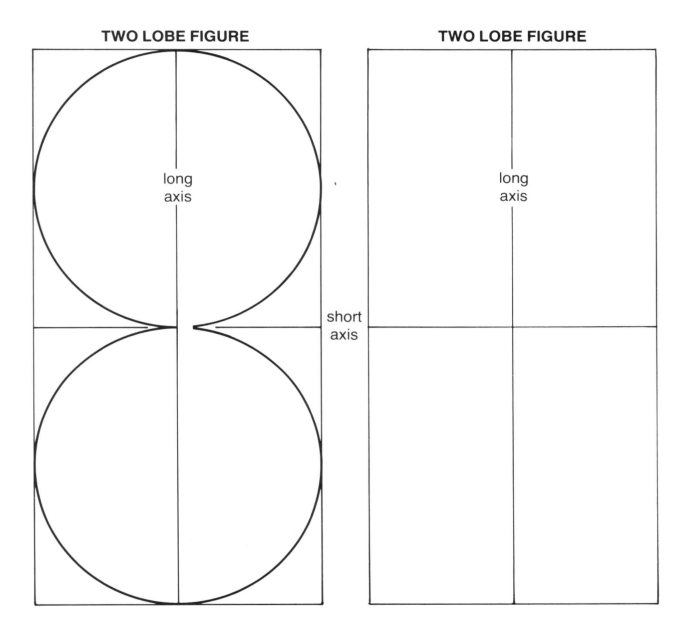

Progress to the next figure on your test and follow the instructions from the previous page: trace the figure on the left (with turns and pushes). Draw your own figure on the right before correcting it with a compass. Imagine how the circle will look before drawing it. Once your pencil is in motion, continue to project the circle in front of the pencil point.

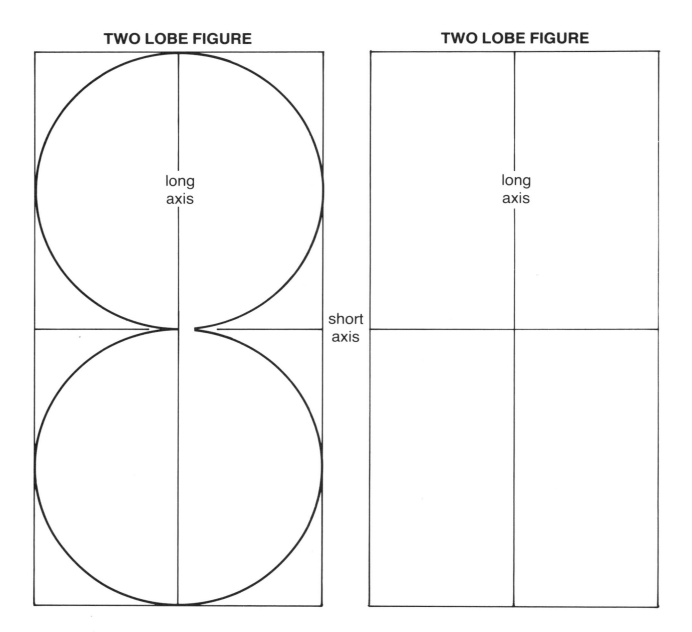

TWO LOBE FIGURE

long
axis

short
axis

TWO LOBE FIGURE

long
axis

Squares are provided on the following pages for two lobe and three lobe figures. Proceed through the figures on your test, drawing one figure per page. Continue until you have an image of each figure from your test. Follow the instructions on page 70. Extra pages have been provided to accommodate those of you who have longer tests.

TWO LOBE FIGURE   ## TWO LOBE FIGURE

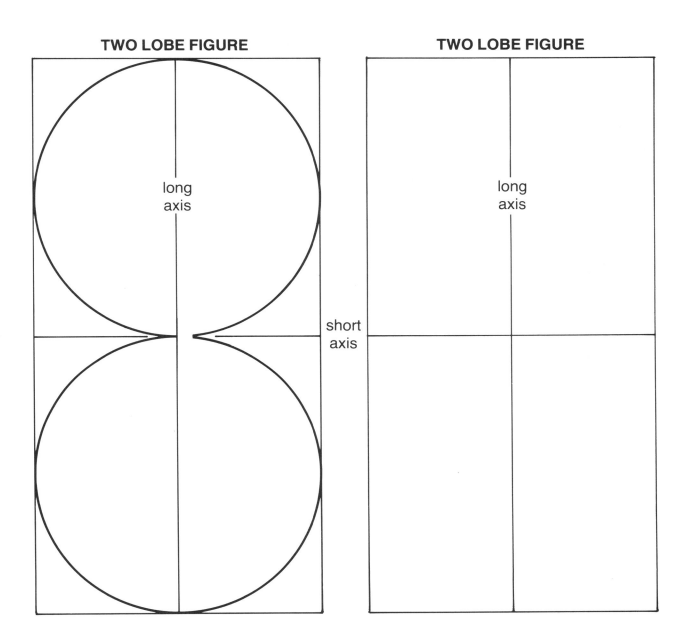

While you skate a figure on the ice, you should always look about 5 to 6 feet (2 meters) in front of your skating foot. When your eyes fall on the Center, stop your eyes and focus on the Point of Pivot until your skating foot turns into the push. As one foot turns into the push, quickly watch the other foot stepping onto the ice. Once on your new skating foot, quickly move your eyes to look 5 to 6 feet (2 meters) ahead. If you follow this procedure, your Centers will be neat and your circles will be better traced.

TWO LOBE FIGURE

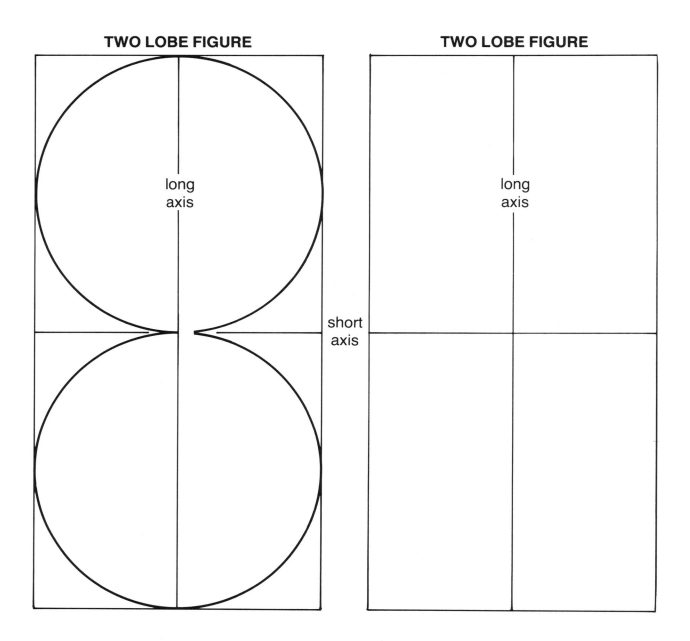

long
axis

short
axis

TWO LOBE FIGURE

long
axis

TWO LOBE FIGURE

TWO LOBE FIGURE

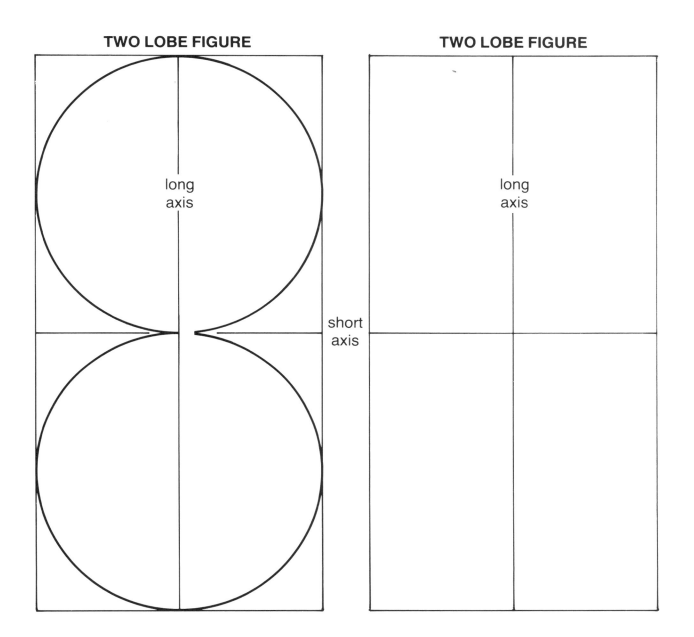

long
axis

short
axis

long
axis

TWO LOBE FIGURE

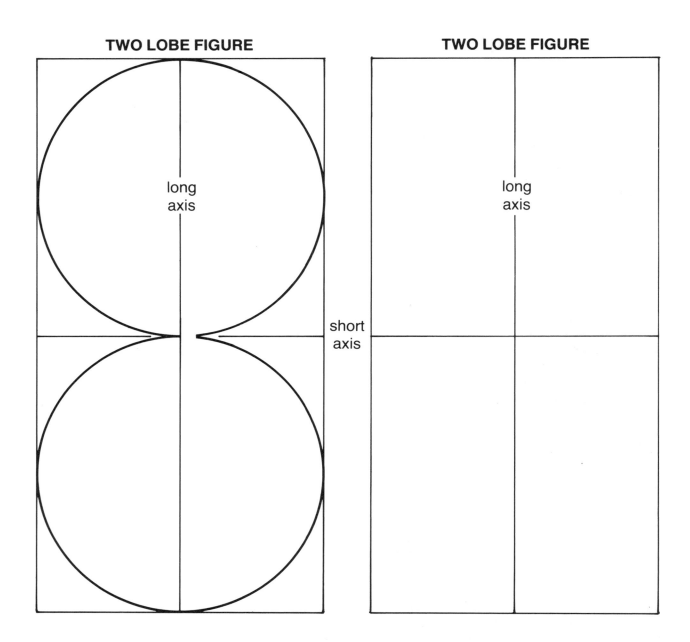

long
axis

short
axis

TWO LOBE FIGURE

long
axis

Draw a serpentine figure on this page just as you would skate it. Trace half a circle, a Change of Edge, and a whole circle. Complete the second half of the figure the same way. Include all the pushes and turns.

THREE LOBE FIGURE   **THREE LOBE FIGURE**

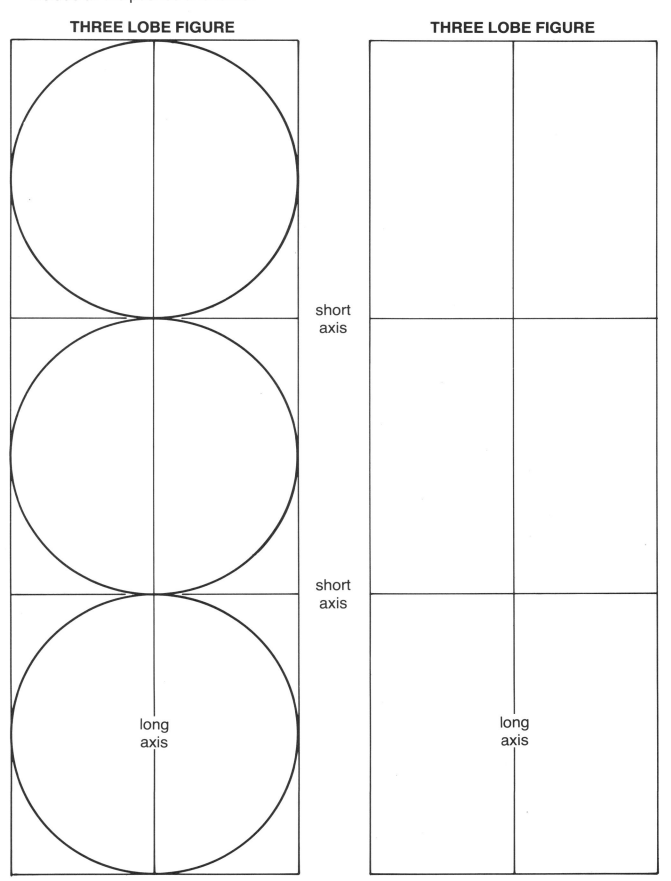

short
axis

short
axis

long
axis

long
axis

THREE LOBE FIGURE

THREE LOBE FIGURE

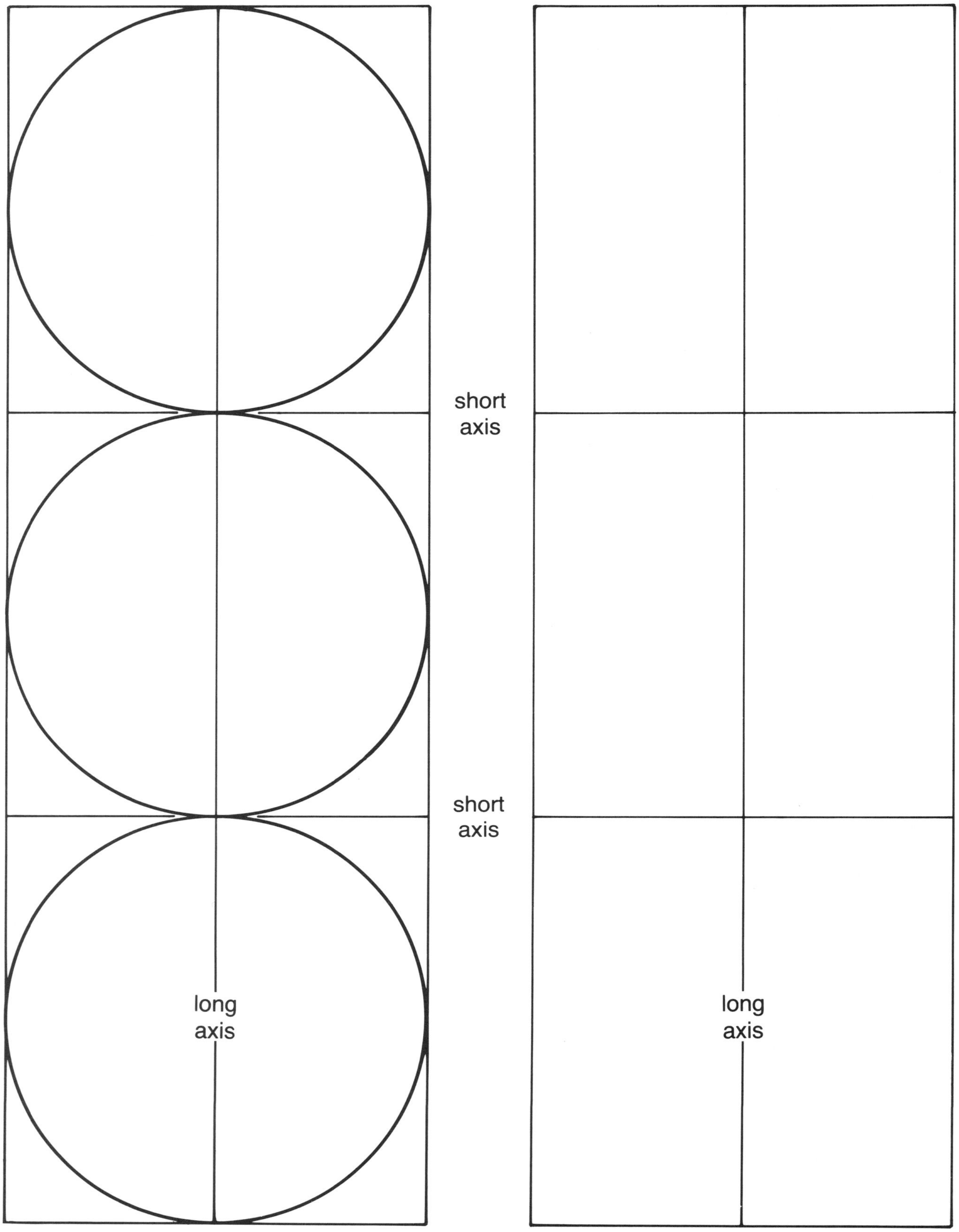

short
axis

short
axis

long
axis

long
axis

78

THREE LOBE FIGURE

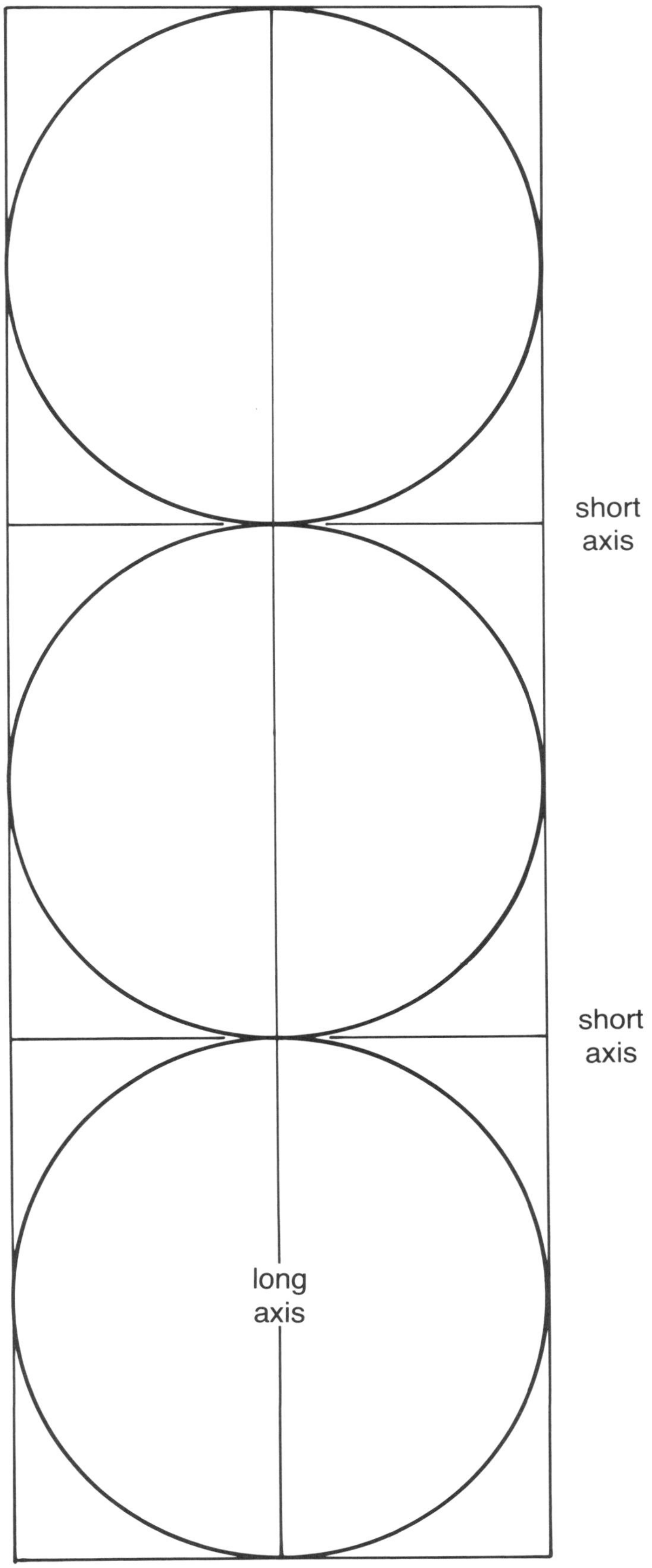

THREE LOBE FIGURE

short
axis

short
axis

long
axis

long
axis

79

THREE LOBE FIGURE

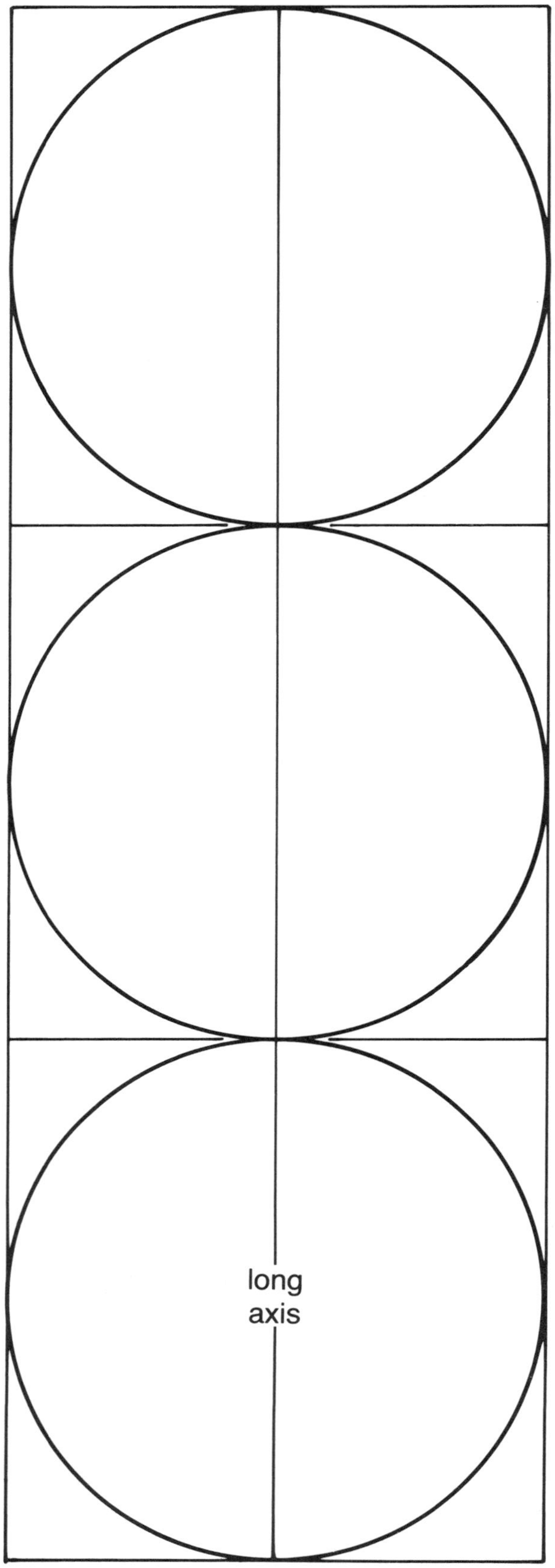

THREE LOBE FIGURE

short
axis

short
axis

long
axis

long
axis

80

THREE LOBE FIGURE

THREE LOBE FIGURE

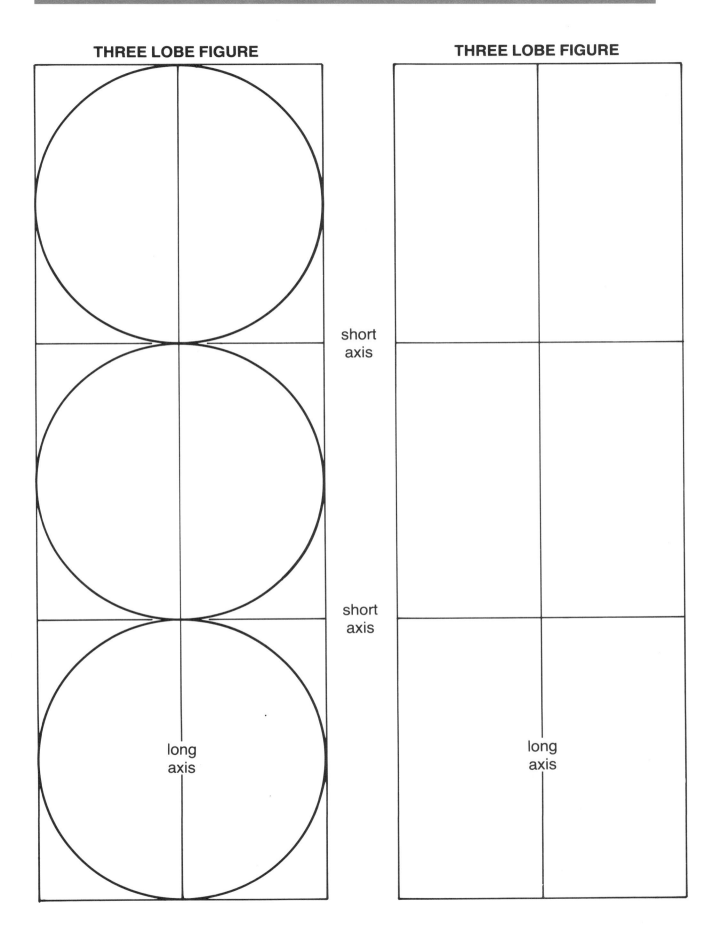

short
axis

short
axis

long
axis

long
axis

THREE LOBE FIGURE

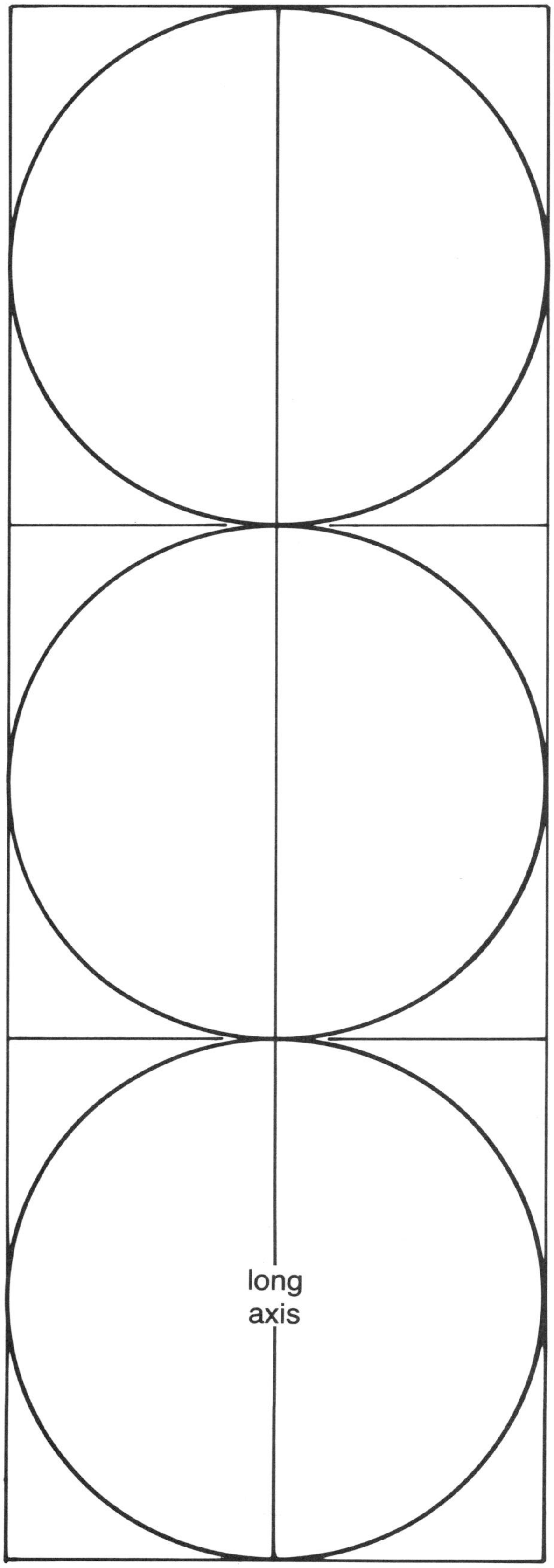

THREE LOBE FIGURE

short
axis

short
axis

long
axis

long
axis

82

Grade Sheet

This is a grade sheet for you to pull out and take to your patch. Ask your coach for permission to skate a three lobe figure on clean ice and to judge the figure according to the sheet. Show your coach the results to see how you are progressing. The concepts on this page are derived from lessons 4 - 8. Center #1 is where you start the figure. Center #2 is the other Center. (Note: you can still use this grade sheet if you don't skate three lobe figures. Just don't fill in the answers for Center #2 questions.)

Centers: Examine your Centers for symmetry.

Center #1: Stand at the long axis. Does the right half look like the left half?

yes   no   *(circle one)*

Stand at the short axis. Does the right half look like the left half?

yes   no   *(circle one)*

The edges into and out of the Center are

clean   short flats   long flats.   *(circle one)*

Center #2: Stand at the long axis. Does the right half look like the left half?

yes   no   *(circle one)*

Stand at the short axis. Does the right half look like the left half?

yes   no   *(circle one)*

The edges into and out of the Center are

clean   short flats   long flats.   *(circle one)*

Changes

Center #1: The Change of Edge is   shaped correctly   S'd   diagonal   *(circle one)*

If the Change of Edge is S'd or diagonal, is it bulged/dented   before   after
on both sides of   the long axis? *(circle one)*

Center #2: The Change of Edge is   shaped correctly   S'd   diagonal   *(circle one)*

If the Change of Edge is S'd or diagonal, is it bulged/dented.   before   after
on both sides of   the long axis? *(circle one)*

Long Axis

Place a guard or a mitten in the middle of the flat on the Change of Edge at each Center to determine the long axis of the change.

The changes are   lined up   off axis. *(circle one)*

Pushes

Center #1: The pushes are at the   correct distance   too early   too late   in relation to the long axis.   *(circle one)*

Center #2: The pushes cross the Change of Edge at the   correct distance   too early   too late   in relation to the long axis.   *(circle one)*

1. When you are laying out a circle on clean ice, what are the two special points that you need to project?

_____

2. By projecting where these two spots are located, you are imagining the first _____ of the circle.

3. When you determine the spot on the ice for the half, you have projected the   width   or   length (circle one) of the circle?

4. Three turns should always point _____ .

5. The shoulders of a three turn should be parallel to _____ .

6. When tracing a figure on ice, you should look 5 or 6 feet (2 meters) in front of your skating foot until you see the Center. Then, where should you look? _____

7. The change in the edge and the _____ must occur simultaneously at the same spot.

8. The _____ axis separates the circle before the Change of Edge from the circle after the Change of Edge.

9. How does a judge examine your circle size? _____

10. Draw a double S'd change.

11. Another name for an oblique change is _____ .
    Draw one.

12. How do you determine the long axis of the Change of Edge?

_____

13. How long should a Change of Edge be on the ice? _____

turn page for answers

Scott Hamilton USA. 1984 Olympic and World Champion
photo by Laura Keesling

Dorothy Hamill USA. 1976 Olympic and World Champion
photo by Frank Heaney

Linda Fratianne USA.
1977 World Champion

QUIZ ANSWERS
LESSONS 7 & 8

1. the quarter and the half
2. half
3. length
4. towards the Center
5. the short axis at the turn
6. at the pushes and stepdowns

7. change of circle
8. short
9. by walking and counting the steps for the length and width of the circle
10.
11. diagonal
12. the center of the flat
13. two blades long

For a change of pace, we are now going to start with circles. Below is a circle with all four quarters marked in place. If you draw two lines connecting these points, they intersect at the very center of the circle. Do this now.

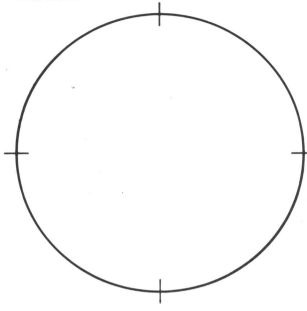

As you know, any line that goes through the center of the circle is a **DIAMETER** of the circle. All diameters of a circle are the same length. One diameter that you drew is the length of the circle and one is the width of the circle. One is parallel to the side of the page and the other is perpendicular to the side of the page.

The center of the circle is the spot where you put the compass or scribe (if you were on the ice). Your scribe is half the length of the diameter. This distance which is ½ the diameter is called the **RADIUS** of the circle.

It's good practice to look at a circle and project where the quarter and half should be. On the circle below, mark the key points of the circle. That is, mark the quarters and the halves. Plan your marks so that if you drew diameters between them, each diameter would be parallel or perpendicular to the side of the page.

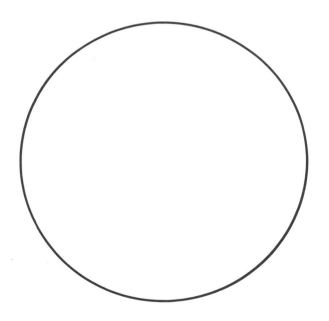

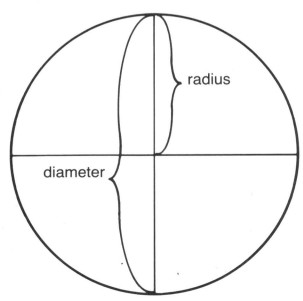

radius

diameter

Cut out one of the plain circles on this page. Use this circle to check the location of the quarter and half marks. Fold the circle four times and mark each crease with your pencil. After you mark in the quarters and halves on the remaining circles on this page, lay the cut out circle over the other circles to see if the marks line up.

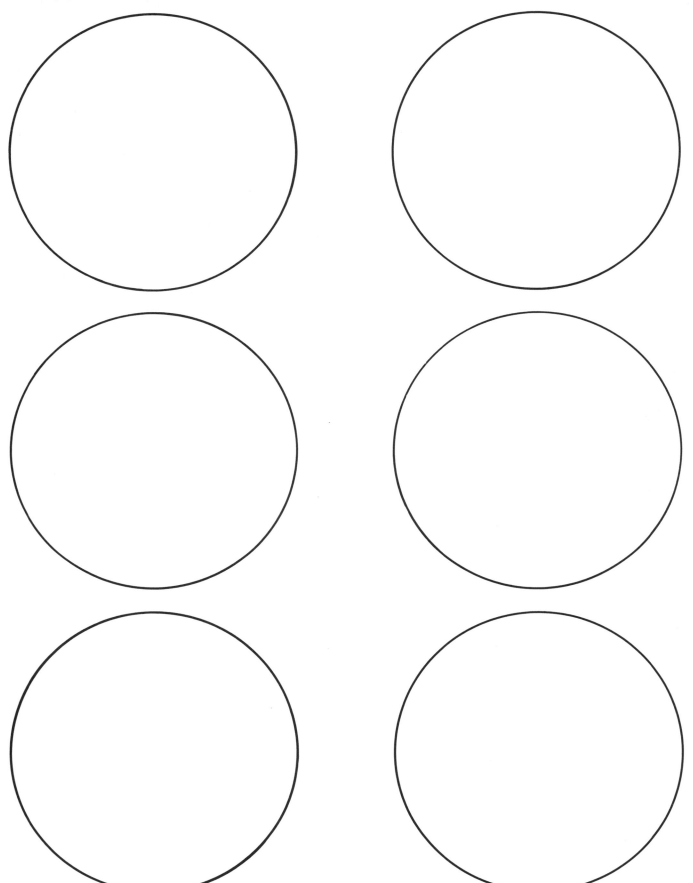

After you have marked the quarters and the halves on these circles, mark in the eighths (halfway between). To check your marks fold your cut out circle one more time, and mark the new creases. Your cut out circle should now have eight marks on it. Lay it over the circles on this page to check the location of the quarters, halves and eighths. Make any necessary corrections.

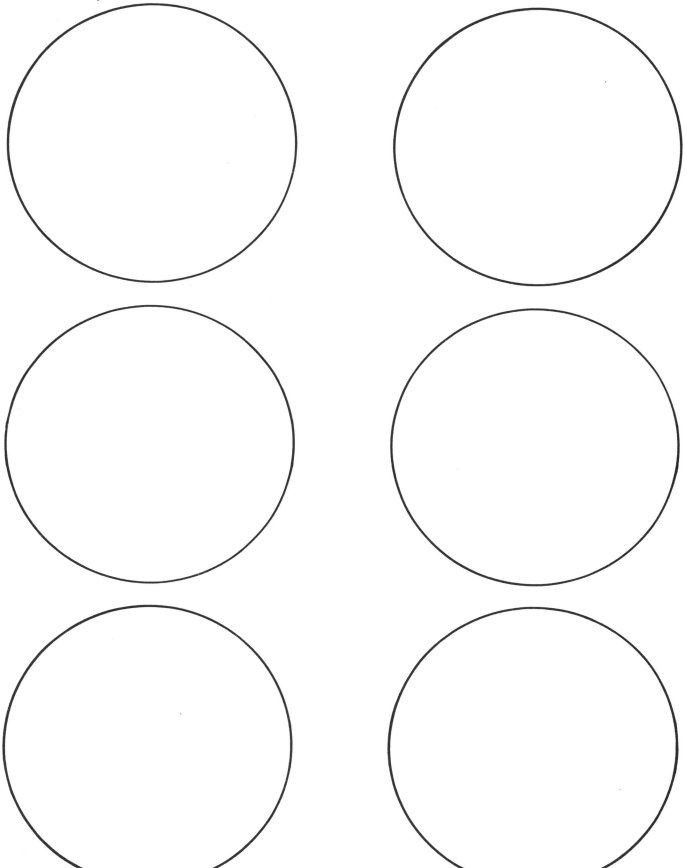

On this page mark the eighths *first* before filling in the quarter and half marks.

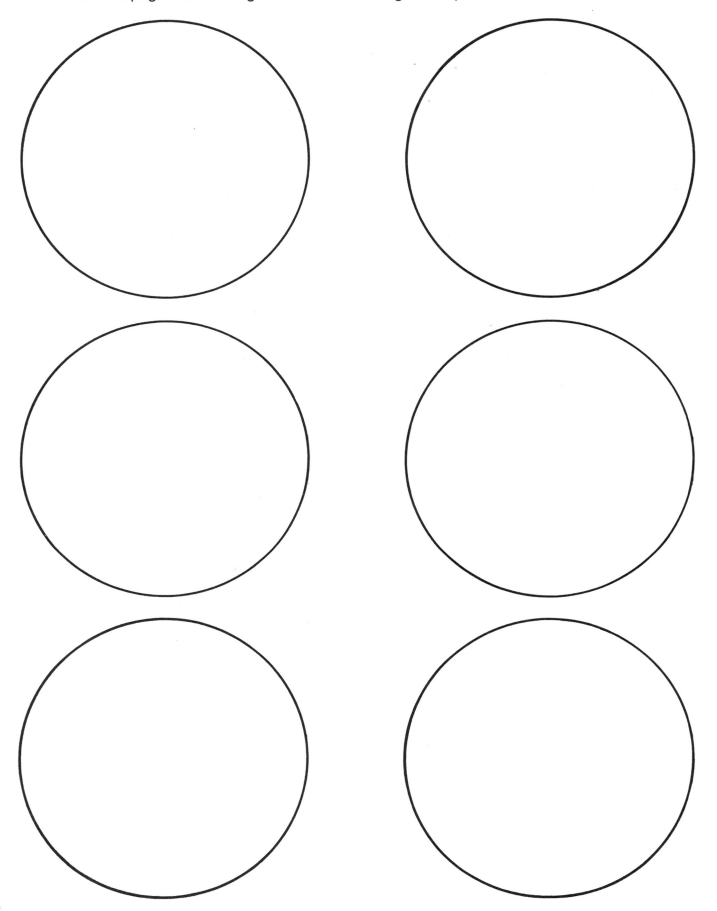

On this page you are going to fill in the blanks: connect the arcs and create a circle. Draw your circles smoothly in the direction indicated by the arrows. This exercise helps you to imagine the curve of the circle before it is drawn in place. Play this game on the ice with your scribe. Just draw small arcs of the circle (instead of the whole thing) and skate in the missing circle. Imagine the path that leads from one arc to the next one.

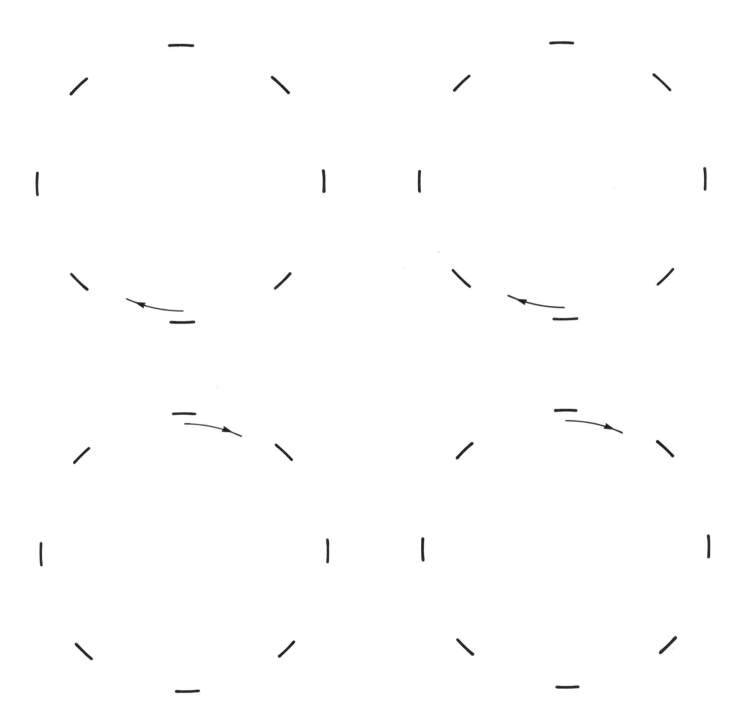

Notice that the arcs drawn below are located on the eighths, the quarters, and the halves. Draw each circle in the direction indicated by the arrow.

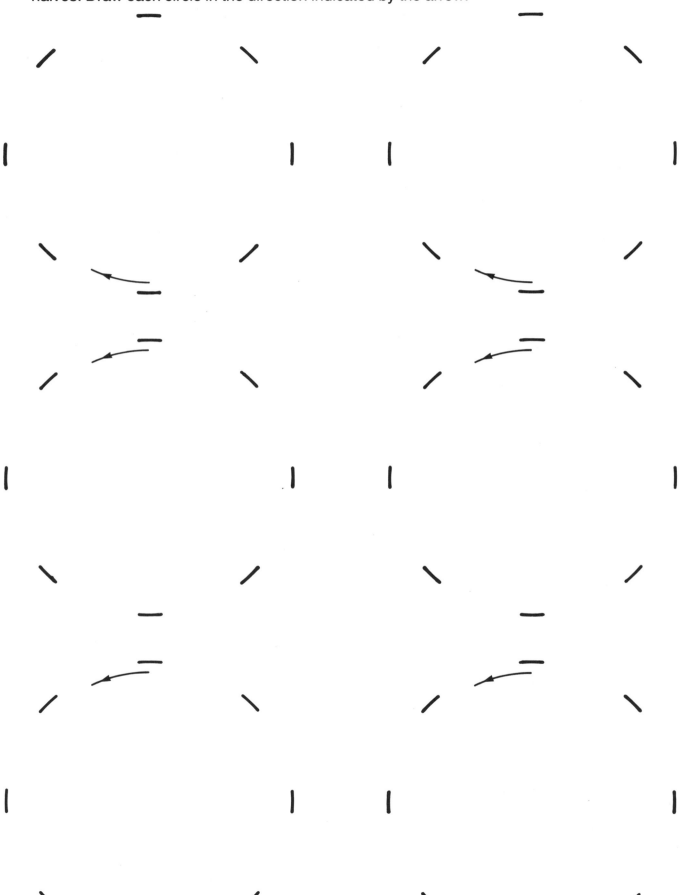

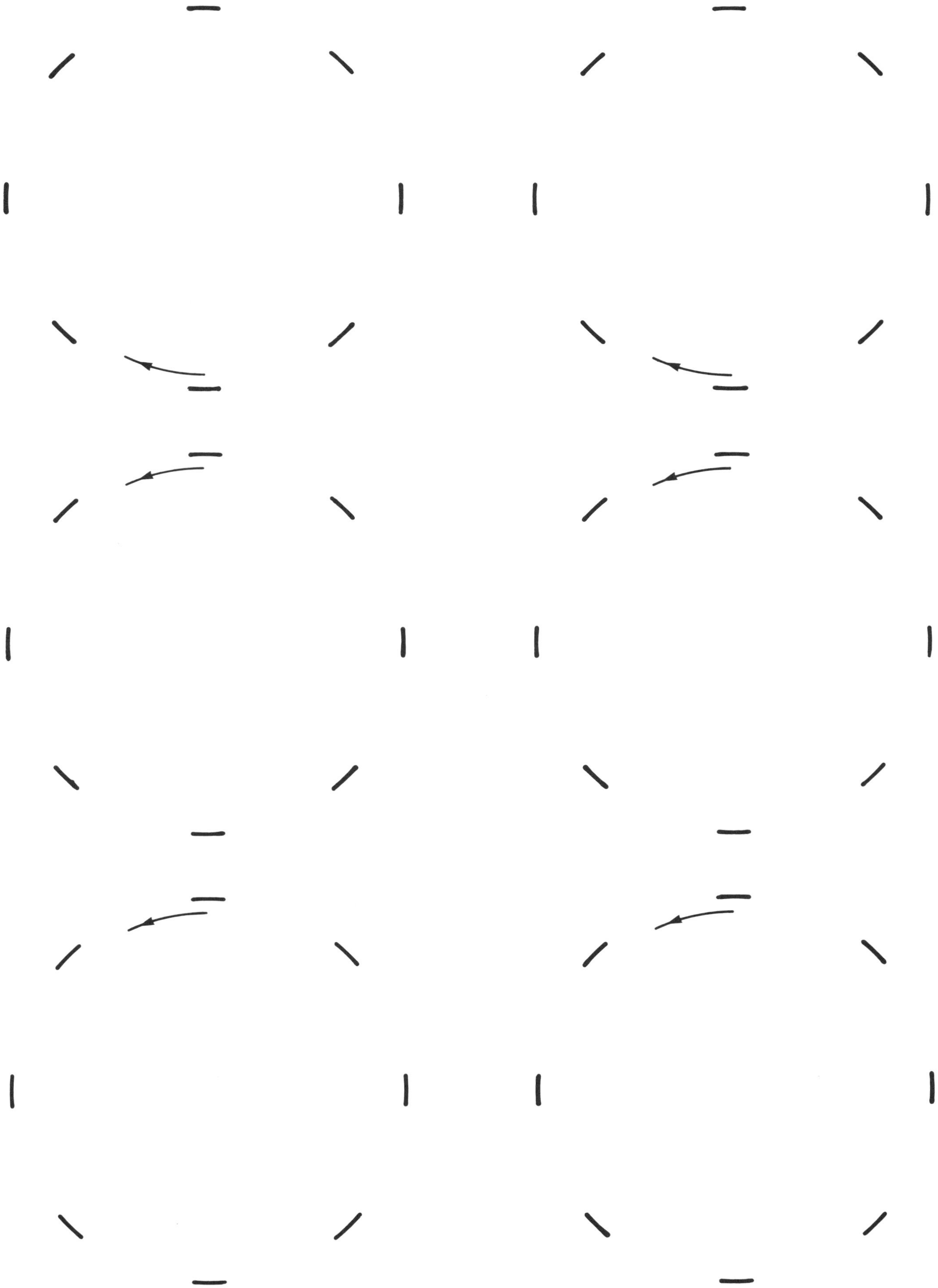

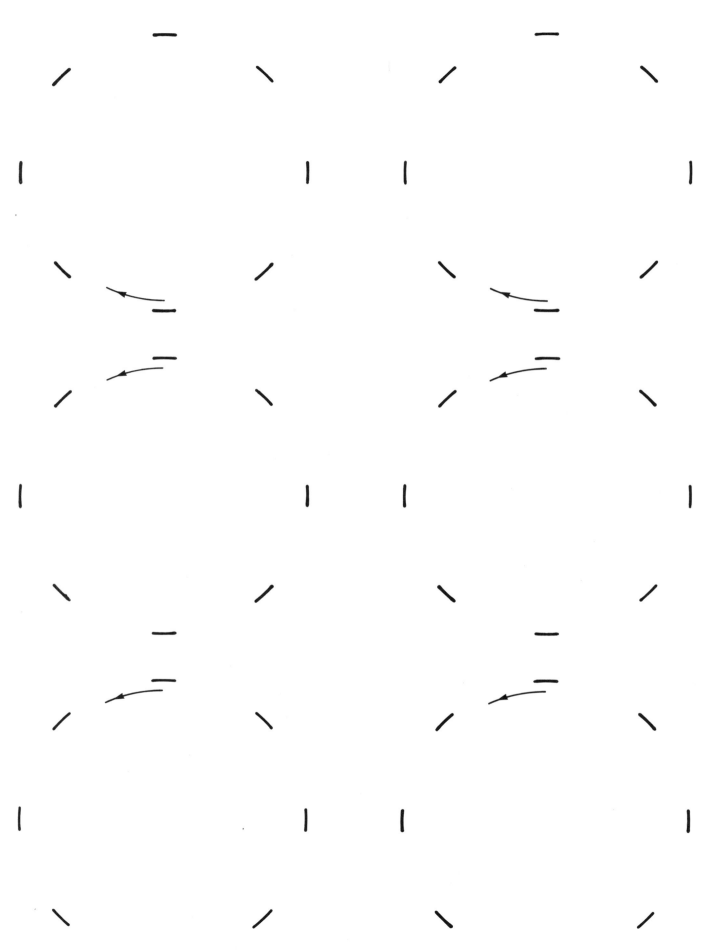

Now we'll give you more challenge: in these exercises only four arcs are provided for you to connect into a good circle. Imagine the path of the missing circle that will lead from one arc to the next one. Draw your circle in the direction indicated by the arrow.

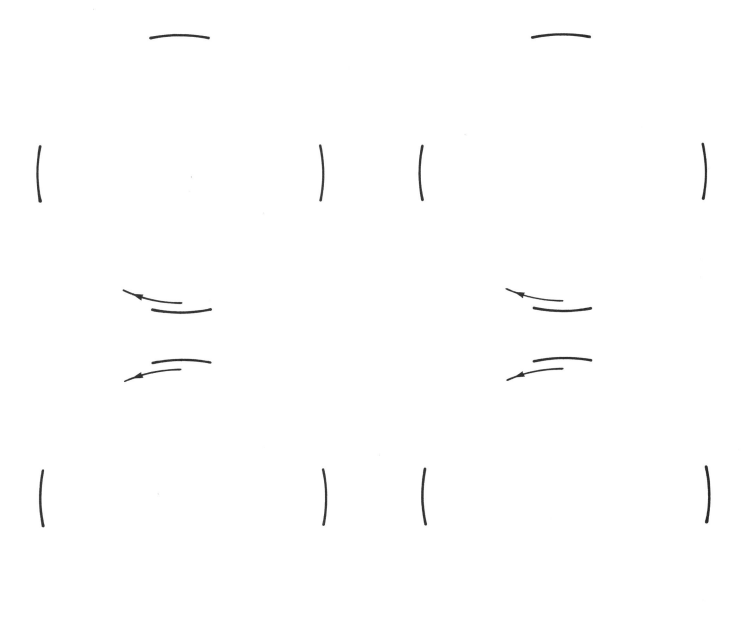

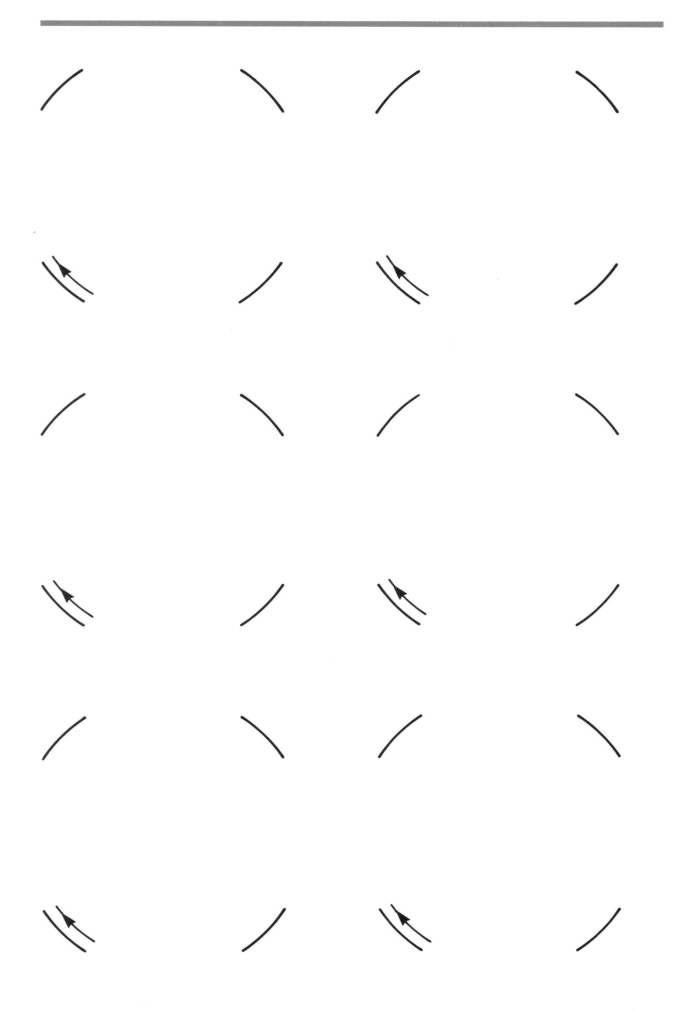

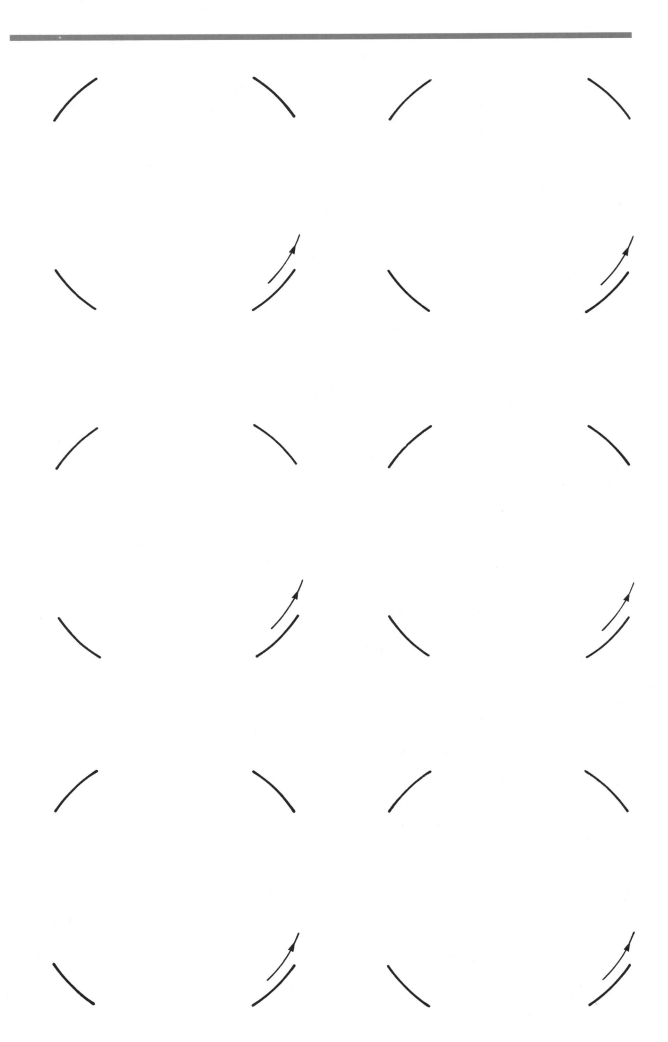

When skating a figure on the ice, the circle always turns in one direction or another. Your head turns in the same direction as the rotation of the circle. Because of the way your head turns, there are **BLIND SPOTS** on the figure that make it difficult to line up the circles. During the first tracing, it is important to look for other key points of the figure in order to line up the quarters. Since the first tracing is the most important one, you should skate it well! Knowing the location of the blind spots will help you to skate your first tracing better.

Imagine you are skating an RFO serpentine like the figure drawn below. This picture illustrates where you are looking at various spots during this serpentine. Let's figure out where the blind spots of the figure are located.

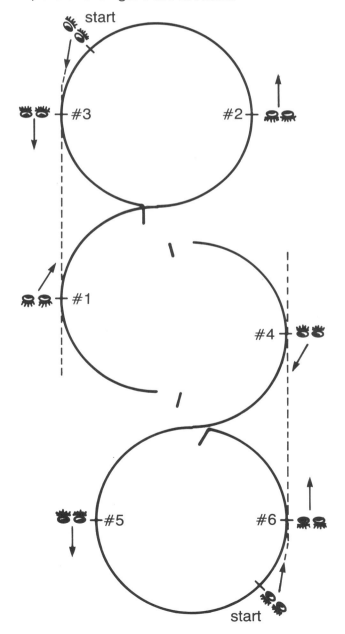

To do this, examine the six places on the serpentine where you strive for line up - the quarters of each circle. If you are unable to see the rest of the figure to judge the line up as you pass through a quarter, we call it a *BLIND SPOT*.

Look at point #1 on the illustration. On the first tracing, no other part of the figure is visible as you pass through point #1. For this reason #1 is a blind spot. Skating through #2 you are also blind because there is no frame of reference on the ice to help you judge the width of the circle. In other words as you skate through the change, you cannot see any other part of the figure to line up point #2.

Before passing through #3 you can start looking down the side of the figure for spot #1 (see illustration). Because you can line up #3 with #1, point #3 is *NOT* blind. As you skate through #4, you can look at the first Center and judge the width of the circle from there. Therefore, point #4 is *NOT* blind.

Skating towards #5, there is nothing on the ice to use to judge the width of the circle. So #5 is blind. Point #6 is a special place because you can view *two* quarters from there. Before reaching #6, begin looking down the side line at both the middle and end circles. Locate points #4 and #2 to judge the line up for the entire right side of the figure.

Which side of the figure has more blind spots? Turn the page and tally the results.

THE RESULTS: On the left side, #1 and #5 are blind. On the right side, #2 is blind.

Since the left side has more blind spots than the right side, the left side is the blind side of the figure. In other words it is harder to line up the left side of the figure. Usually the first side of the figure is the harder side to line up, as you saw on this serpentine.

You can adjust for blind spots on a figure once you know where they are. Here are some tricks for lining up the blind side of the figure:

1. Since point #1 on the previous page is a blind spot, compensate for this before you push off for the first tracing. While standing at your Center, use your mental picture and imagine where the path of the circle will fall at the 1st quarter. You've been practicing this on paper so you can visualize this on the ice.

2. It is possible (although risky) to use the boards as a point of reference when skating through the Change of Edge to point #5 on the illustration.

3. If there is any kind of line on the ice, always start your figure by skating towards the line. This way if your 1st quarter falls 12 inches (26 cms.) away from a hockey line, then each circle should fall the same distance from the line. Do not start a figure so the quarter of the circle is any closer to a painted line than 12 inches (26 cms.). Besides hockey lines there are other kinds of lines on the ice: the side of another figure or patch creates a "line" on its side line. If that line is straight, use it to judge your own figure.

4. The ice usually has variations in color. Learn to use dark spots on the ice to place key circle points. For example, when choosing your starting spot, line up with a dark splotch so that the turn, the half, or the Change of Edge fall on that spot.

Other hints for laying out figures on the ice include the following:

1. Memorize the length of your circles. Learn to stand at the Center, look up the long axis and mentally measure the distance for the length of your circle. Pick a spot for the half of your circle. Skate to that spot. Then check your circle length with the scribe to see if you were correct. You should be correct within 3 inches (6-7 cms.).

2. Know that the Zamboni also leaves lines on the ice. Sometimes these lines are from the Zamboni blade that cuts the ice and other times the lines are from the water as it freezes. The Zamboni lines are usually parallel to the short axis of a figure and appear as a color variation.
Water lines occur when the water spreads out, stops and freezes in an uneven surface. Be careful! Try not to skate turns or Centers on water lines: the water on one side of the line can freeze at a different level from the water on the other side. The ridge that results can throw you off balance or create flats.

3) **Always clean the snow off your blades before skating a figure.** Snow on your blades can cause water marks on turns that look like flats. You don't want points deducted from your score for flats if they were really water marks. Do yourself a favor. *CLEAN YOUR BLADES* before every figure when testing and competing!

It's time to lay out each figure on your test, one by one. You will start by drawing three tracings for each figure in a square on the left. Try to improve your circle and Center with each tracing. Where you like the first tracing, try to copy it exactly by superimposing the second and third tracing directly on top of the first one. Each repeat tracing is called a **SUPERIMPOSITION** because you lay it over the first tracing. After drawing your figure, check it by using a compass. Trace the corrected circle. On the right side of the page lay out your figure without the aid of any lines.

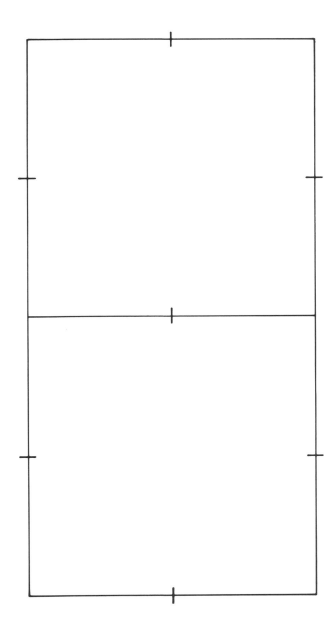

On the following pages squares are drawn for each figure on your test. Draw three tracings in the squares, correct them with a compass, and trace the scribed circle. A space is provided for your layout on the right. Use all the techniques we have learned to correctly judge your circle. Project where you want the side line to be before your first tracing so both circles will be the same width. Ask yourself the following questions after your layout: 1. Are your circles round?
2. Are both circles the same size? width and length?
3. Are your circles lined up on the sides?
4. Are your turns (if any) in the right place? and
5. Are your circles on the same long axis?
The more often you answer "yes" to these questions, the better your figures are drawn.

Correct your layout by drawing circles with the compass. Note how the scribed circle differs from drawn circles. Trace the correct circle 3 times before going on to the next page.

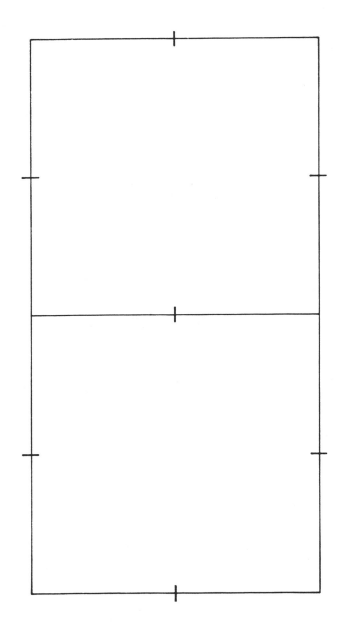

Continue with the next figure on your test. After going through the steps outlined on the previous page, ask yourself the following questions.

1. Are your circles round?
2. Are both circles the same? width and length?
3. Are your circles lined up on the sides?
4. Are your turns (if any) in the right place?
5. Are your circles on the same long axis?

If you answered no to any of these questions, try to prevent that problem from occurring on the next pages.

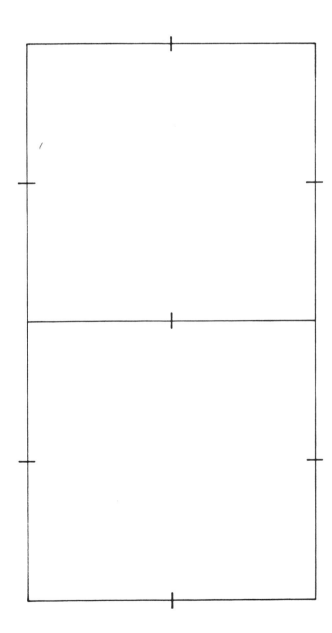

Move on to the next figure on your test. Draw a practice figure on the left and a freehand figure on the right. Correct each one with the compass and trace the corrections.

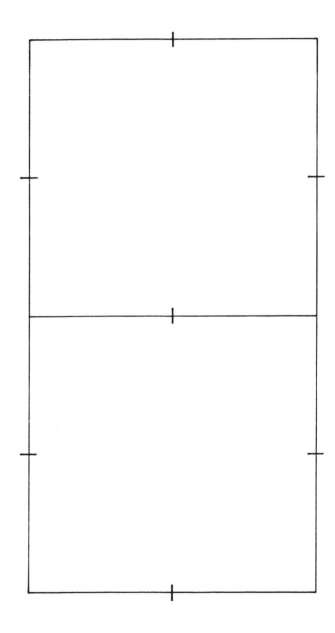

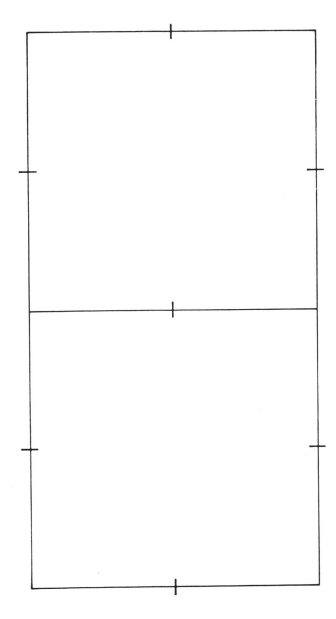

Squares are provided on this page for a three lobe figure or serpentine. Draw a practice figure on the left and correct it with the compass. Trace the corrections. Lay out the figure on the right. Again use the compass and follow the corrected tracing 3 times.

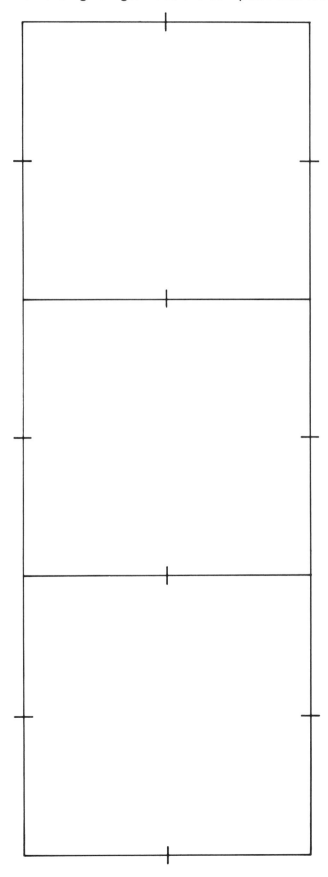

Answer the following questions after drawing your layout circles on the right.
1. Are your circles round?
2. Are all three circles the same?   width and length?
3. Are your circles lined up on the sides?
4. Are your turns (if any) in the right place?
5. Are your circles on the same long axis?

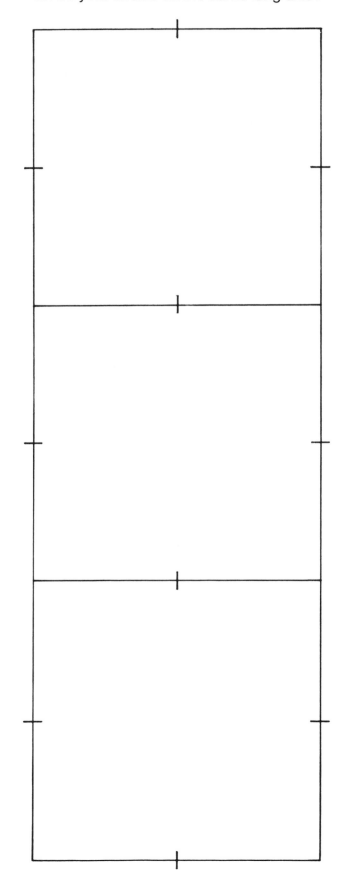

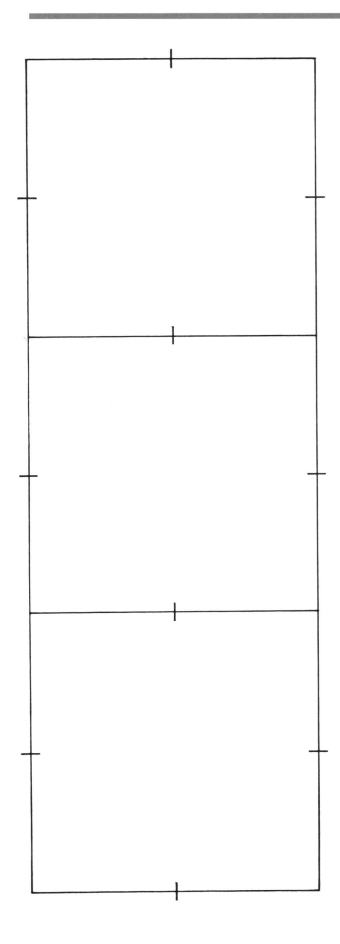

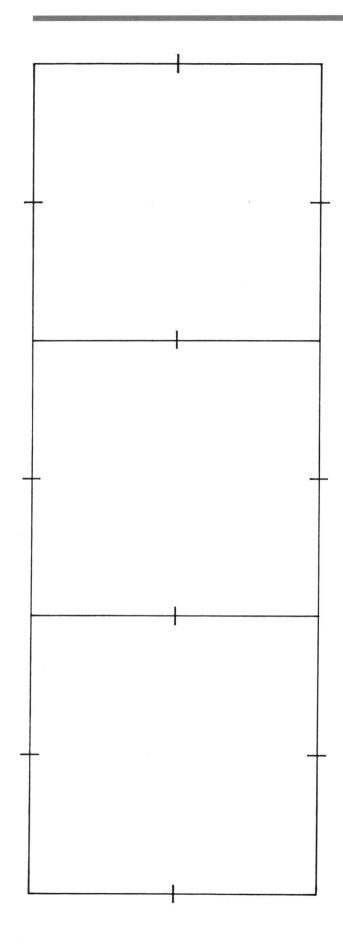

1. A word that refers to the second and third tracing of a figure is _____.

2. List three things to look for after skating a layout of a figure:

a: _____

b: _____

c: _____

3. The _____ of the circle is any line that goes through the center of the circle while connecting the edges of the circle.
Choose one: side line
        arc
        radius
        diameter
        axis

4. The compass or scribe is extended to a distance which is half the length of the circle. This distance, which is the length of the scribe, is called the _____ of the circle. (choose a word from #3)

5. The diameter that connects the halves of the circle is equal in length to the diameter that connects the 1st and 3rd quarter of the circle. (true or false)

6. Which side of the figure is usually the "blind" side? _____

7. You are about to lay out a figure on a test and you are going to use a patch with a hockey line on one side. Should you start facing towards or away from the line? _____

8. How far should your tracing fall from the hockey line in the example above? _____

turn page for answers   **111**

John Curry GBR. 1976 Olympic and World Champion
photo by Fred Dean

Rosalynn Sumners USA.
1983 World Champion
1984 Olympic Silver Medalist
photo by Don Borman

Kira Ivanova USSR.
1984 Olympic Bronze Medalist
photo by Fred Dean

QUIZ ANSWERS
LESSONS 9 and 10

1. superimposition
2. circle shape, circle size, circle line up
3. diameter
4. radius
5. true
6. the side you face as you start
7. towards the line
8. more than 12 inches (26 cms.) away

Now its time to get your scissors ready! Cut out the squares below and cut a circle out of each square. The marks on the inside of each square will help you cut a better circle. Compare your circles to the one drawn in the square below. Notice how much better your circles are now compared to the first time you did this exercise. Save these circles.

LESSON
11
Overlapping Circles

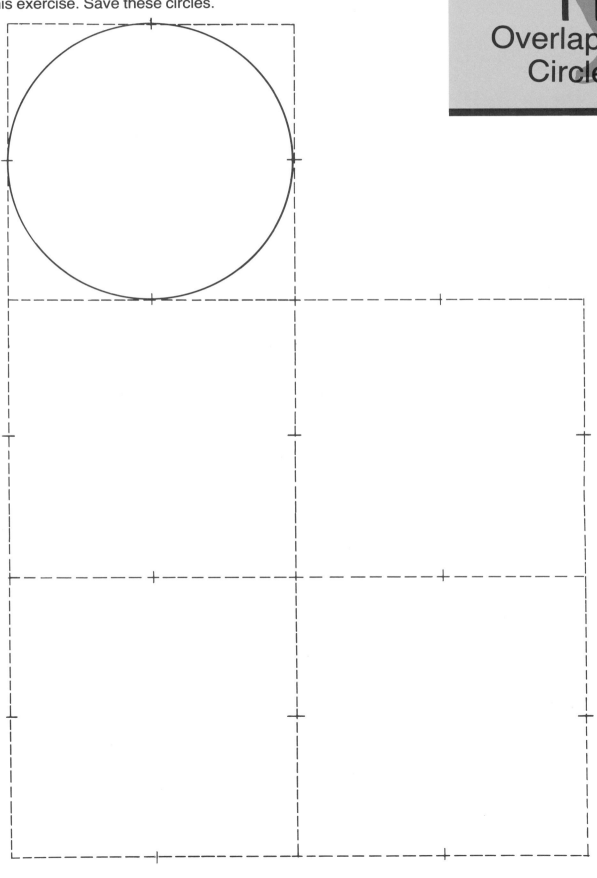

Instead of having marks drawn at each quarter, only the halves are marked on this page. Cut out these squares and see how well you cut out these circles. Picture in your mind where the circle will touch the side of the square. Keep these circles so you can create figure eights.

With no lines to assist you, cut out the best circles you can from the squares you cut out below. Now you are going to create a patch with your cut out circles. Take two white circles that you cut out. Lay them on the desk in front of you so they just touch, forming a figure eight. Using two red circles, arrange them so they form a figure eight. Place them on top of the first eight *ONLY SLIGHTLY MOVED UP* from the first figure.

Continue to place cut out figure eights on top of the previous ones creating a picture like illustration #1 on page 6. Alternate red and white eights. Be sure to put three circles together to make a serpentine. Lay these on your patch too. Line up the sides of the circles.

Below you see two overlapping figure eights. On Drawing #1 examine the figure shown in black. Follow around the black circles with your pencil as you would skate them. Points A, B, C, and D all fall where the quarters of the circle touch the side lines.

Prepare to trace the figure in red on Drawing #1. The red Center is 1 inch (2.56 cms.) from the black Center. As your pencil moves toward   point E on the red figure, it passes to the *inside* of point B on the black figure. On the side line the quarter of the red circle (E) is 1 inch (2.56 cms.) from the quarter of the black circle (B). When your pencil reaches the half of the red circle, it too is 1 inch (2.56 cms.) from the black circle, just like the Centers and all of the quarters. Draw through the Center and onto the second circle of the red figure. After point G, notice how the circle curves to the *inside* of point D on the black figure.

On drawing #2 the red figure isn't lined up with the black figure. In this case the red circle is drawn *through* point B of the black circle instead of passing to the *inside* of it. This error destroys the side line up and tends to shift the whole circle to the right. Then, point F is no longer in the right location either.

The second circle is off axis too. This circle is too wide at the quarter and passes *through* point D on its way to the half (instead of passing to the inside). Then the circle is too long and the last quarter is out of line.

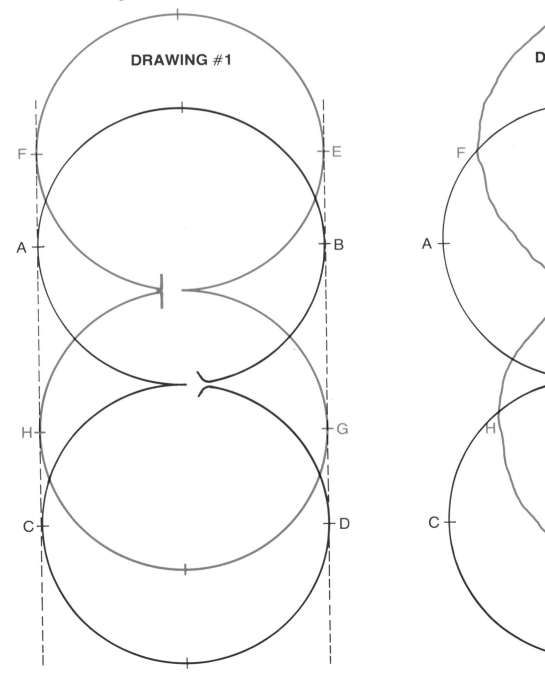

DRAWING #1

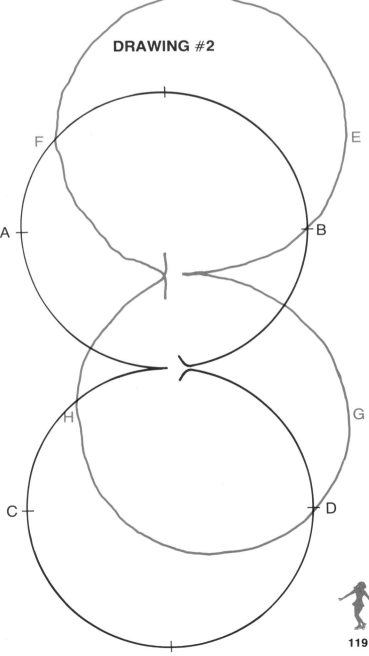

DRAWING #2

By drawing figures inside of each other on paper, you can prevent these mistakes from happening on the ice. On this page the first figure is drawn on each patch. Draw the second figure on the same long axis. Make corrections with your compass and trace them. When skating the second figure, one circle falls *outside* of and the other circle falls *inside* of the circle of the previous figure. However, on both circles the tracing passes to the *inside* of the quarter of the previous figure.

When the Centers are 1 inch (2.5 cms.) apart, then the tops of the circles should also be 1 inch (2.5 cms) apart. Figure out where your circle will hit the side line before drawing each circle.

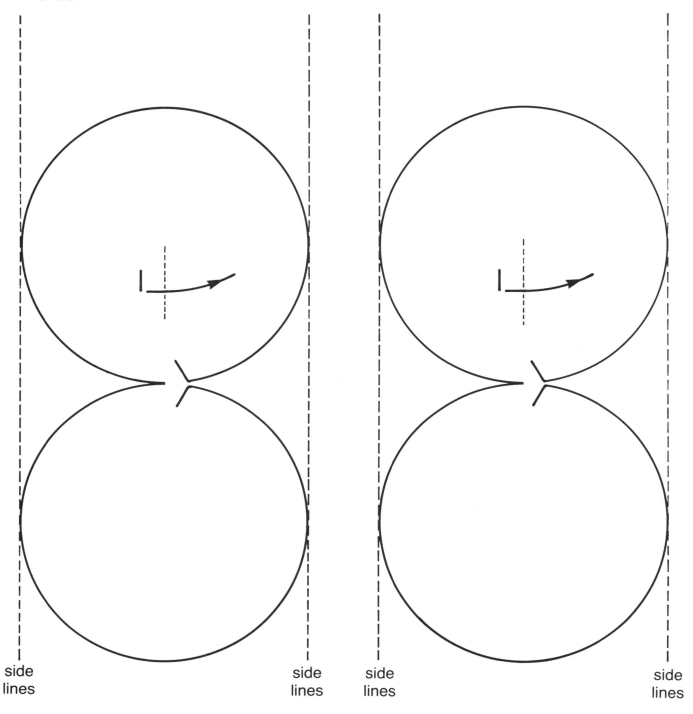

side
lines

side
lines

side
lines

side
lines

The principles of drawing figures inside of each other (as you are doing) apply to all figures that are drawn on the same long axis. These rules also apply on the ice. Serpentines, threes, and basic eight's all follow the same four principles of layout on the ice: **1)** The distance between the Centers equals the distance between the halves. When the halves move up 3 feet (92 cms.), the quarters move 3 feet (92 cms.) up the side lines. **2)** The quarters of the circle should all fall on the same line which is the side line of the patch. **3)** One circle always falls *outside* of the previous figure and the other circle always falls *inside* of the previous figure. **4) ALWAYS** skate to the *inside* of the quarter of the previous figure. **NEVER** skate *through* the quarter of the previous figure.

After drawing the second figure in the illustration on the left, try it without the help of any lines in the figure on the right.

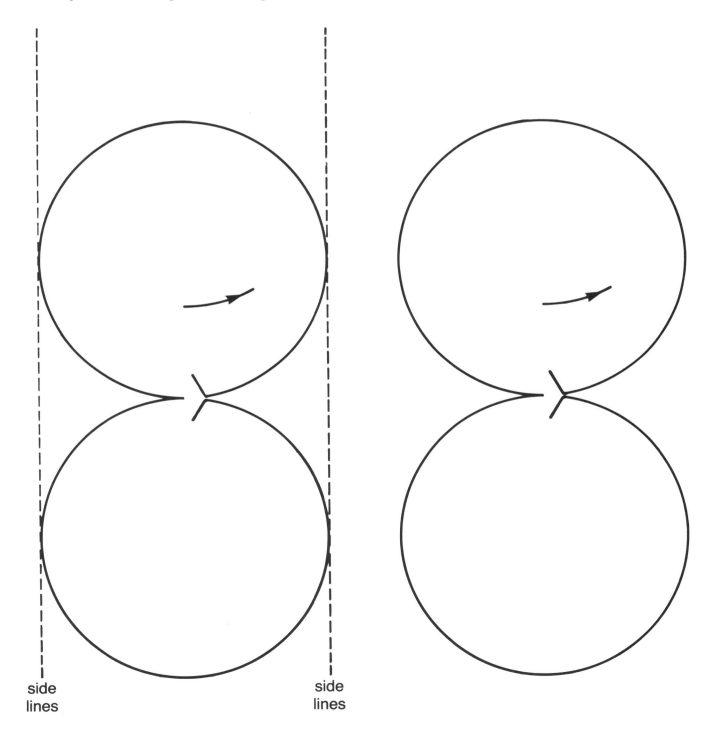

side
lines

side
lines

Now practice below without the aid of any lines.

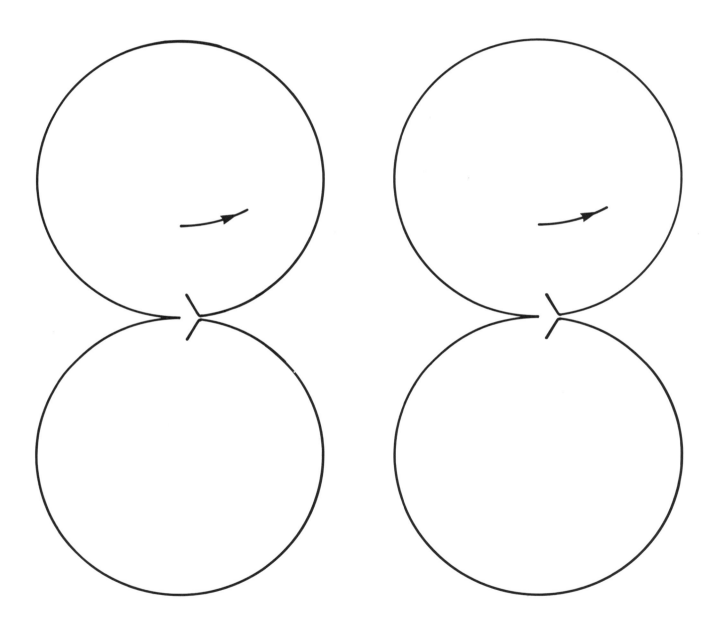

LESSON 12
Three Turns

In order to discuss three turns, you need to understand the blade and its edges first. Some skaters use the same "all purpose" blade for compulsory figures as they do freestyle. At some point as you advance with skating, it is recommended to own a special pair of boots and blades just for figures. A figure blade differs from an all purpose blade in three ways: 1) A figure blade has a greater curvature along the length of the blade. The additional rock to the blade makes turning on the figure an easier process. 2) The bottom toe pick has been removed from a figure blade to facilitate the rocking motion in turns. 3) A figure blade is ground with a very shallow hollow between the edges. This increases the glide of the blade across the ice (by reducing friction).

A **THREE TURN** is a turn from forwards to backwards (or vice versa) on one foot. It is a turn on one lobe from an edge of one character to an edge of the opposite character. In other words there is a change of edge in the middle of the turn. To change the edge, your blade first tilts to one side, then rolls up to a flat in the middle, and finally leans over to the other side. **A three turn always turns from a circle to the same circle.**

When are you supposed to change the edge? At the top of course! During a RFO three turn your foot turns a half rotation from forwards to backwards. This half rotation can be divided into two parts. The first ¼ rotation is on an outer edge and the second ¼ rotation is on an inner edge. In the middle of the turn your foot should be pointing directly down the long axis towards the Center. As you already know, to change the tilt of your blade from an outside to an inside edge you must roll your foot over the "flat" in the middle.

A perfect three turn has a flat at the tip of the turn exactly as narrow as your blade. This tiny gap at the tip of the turn makes this an **OPEN TOPPED** turn. A three turn can be **CLEAN** without being open topped. A clean three turn just isn't as light or quick as an open topped one. But, no flat or change of edge is visible on a clean three turn - only crisp edges are visible.

Three turn mistakes fall into four catagories:

1) SHAPE ERRORS: the shoulders of the turn are uneven, not symmetrical, and not parallel to the short axis at the turn.

2) PRESSURE ERRORS: too little or too much pressure creates lines that are either invisible or too thick (scraped) on the ice.

3) EDGE ERRORS: the edge changes too early or too late.

4) PLACEMENT ERRORS: the turns are too early or too late on the circle in relation to the long axis. Misplaced turns usually point in the wrong direction.

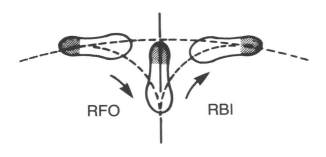

RFO   RBI

SHAPE & PRESSURE ERRORS

Lets's examine the four types of three turn errors. The mistakes illustrated on this page are either shape or pressure mistakes. Grades are assigned to three turns on a scale from A to F, where A is excellent. Grades of C, D, or F fail tests. The grades given below apply only if the turn is also clean. An additional edge problem on any of these turns would change the grade accordingly. Since mistakes like to travel in groups of two or three, it is often possible to correct an edge problem by correcting the shape or placement of the turn.

GRADE

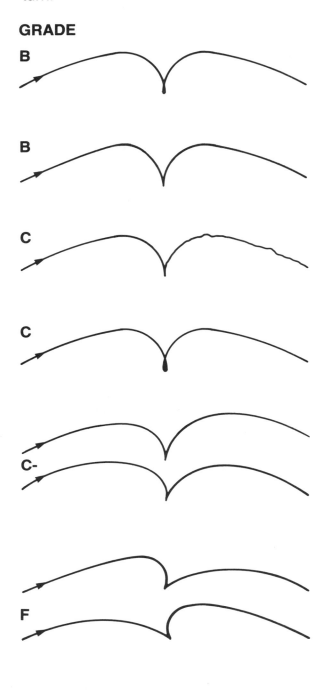

B

B

C

C

C-

F

TYPE OF TURN

LITE SPOON: This is a small scooped out area the size of a little fingernail occurring at the tip of a turn. It is caused by too much pressure at the top of the turn.

DENT ON SHOULDER OF TURN: A flattening of the curve of the circle skated before or after the turn creates this shape problem.

WOBBLES AFTER TURNS: This results from a loss of balance during and after the turn.

HEAVY SPOON: This appears as a scooped out area about the size of a small spoon at the tip of the turn. The edge before the turn creates the spoon because it is pressed too hard and held too long.

UNEVEN SHOULDERS TO THE TURN: The shoulders of the turn are not parallel to the short axis at the turn. This shape error causes edge problems and placement problems.

HOOKED OR BEAKED TURNS: A turn curling in one direction or another so it no longer points down the long axis. This mistake comes from pulling your foot around the turn. There are two versions of this error: **OVER ROTATED** and **UNDER ROTATED**. An over rotated turn means that your skating foot has curved too far in the direction of rotation before turning backwards. An under rotated turn indicates that your foot hasn't curved around enough before turning backwards.

EDGE ERRORS

The third type of three turn mistake relates to the edge and when the edge changes. This page has diagrams of three turns - good ones and bad ones. These three turns are each assigned a grade. The mistakes illustrated on this page are graded as if there are only edge errors on the turn. Additional shape problems would lower the grade.

GRADE

A +

A

B

C-

D

F

F

TYPE OF TURN

OPEN TOPPED: Ideally the edge changes at the tip of the turn. This change is so quick and light that a hairline gap less than the width of the blade is left on the ice.

CLEAN: The edge changes at the right spot but without the quickness or lightness of the open topped turn.

SHORT FLATS: A double line the width of the blade occuring on one side of the turn. Any flat less than 2 inches (5 cms.) long on the ice is considered short.

LONG FLAT ON ONE SIDE: Any flat 3 inches (8 cms.) or longer is considered long on the ice. Your foot is not tilting enough to feel the edges.

LONG FLATS ON BOTH SIDES: Flats over 3 inches (8 cms.) on both sides of the turn mean your foot is straight instead of tilted during the turn.

CHANGED TURN: The edge changes *too late* because the edge before the turn is held too long. The tilt of the blade is correct but the roll of the foot needs to occur sooner.

CHANGED TURN: The edge changes *too early*. A change of edge before the turn is worse than a change of edge after the turn. When the change is early, you have no feel for the edges of the turn and no idea when the edge should change. Whenever the top of a three turn is filled in, a red flag should go up in your mind. The scrape that fills in the top of a turn indicates a change of edge before the turn.

If the edge changes more than 4 inches (10 cms.) before or after a turn, or if there is a skid across the top of a turn, the error is so bad it isn't even on this grading scale!

PLACEMENT ERRORS

The last category of three turn errors refers to where the turn is located on the circle. Below we have illustrated placement problems.

GRADE

C   F

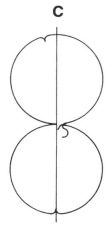 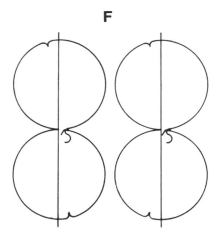

TYPE OF ERROR

ONE TURN EARLY OR LATE: One turn is off axis. In the three turn figure shown the turn is not on the same long axis as the Center.

TWO TURNS OFF AXIS: Turns are on a different long axis than that of the Center.

Here are some examples of how one mistake creates others.

A hooked turn is often changed early. Sometimes it is also placed too early in relation to the long axis.

A spooned turn is often flat on the second side and too heavy or scraped on the first side of the turn.

Early turns frequently have uneven shoulders and a flat or change of edge before the turn.

Late turns often have uneven shoulders and sometimes look beaked. The edge usuallly changes late also.

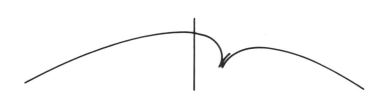

1. What is an A+ turn called and what does it look like (draw it) ?

_____

2. You have just skated one figure on a patch and you are about to skate the second figure two feet (60 cms.) away from the first Center. What should the distance between the two circles be at the top or half of the circle? _____

What should the distance between the quarters be? _____

3. In order to keep the sides of your figure lined up with the first figure skated, always skate to the _____ of the 1st quarter of the previous circle.

4. List three types of errors that can occur on three turns besides the problem of changing the edge at the proper spot?

a) _____ b) _____ c) _____

5. Draw a spooned three turn.

6. Draw a beaked turn.

7. Draw a three turn where the edge changes too early.

8. What creates a curve and an edge? _____

Katarina Witt GDR. 1984 Olympic Champion
and World Champion
photo by Fred Dean

Denise Biellmann SWI.
1981 World Champion
photo by Fred Dean

Janet Lynn USA.
1972 Olympic Bronze Medalist
photo courtesy Janet Lynn

Robin Cousins GBR. 1980 Olympic Champion
photo by Fred Dean

QUIZ ANSWERS
LESSONS 11 and 12

1. open topped

2. two feet (52 cms.), two feet (52 cms.)
3. inside
4. a. shape   b. pressure   c. placement

5.

6.

7.

8. the lean of your body and the tilt of your foot.

On the following pages we have drawn the first few figure tests as they would be laid out on a patch for the test. Each test is marked as ISIA, USFSA or CFSA. Find the test you are working on and study that page.

USFSA and CFSA PRELIMINARY FIGURE TEST AND ISIA FIGURE 1.

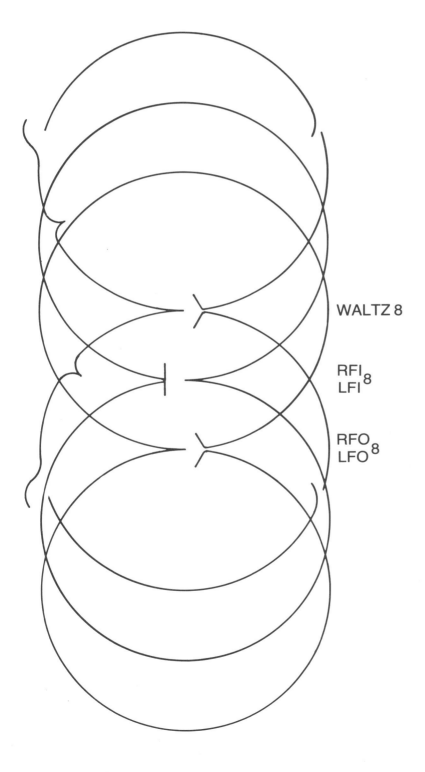

WALTZ 8

RFI$_8$
LFI^8

RFO$_8$
LFO^8

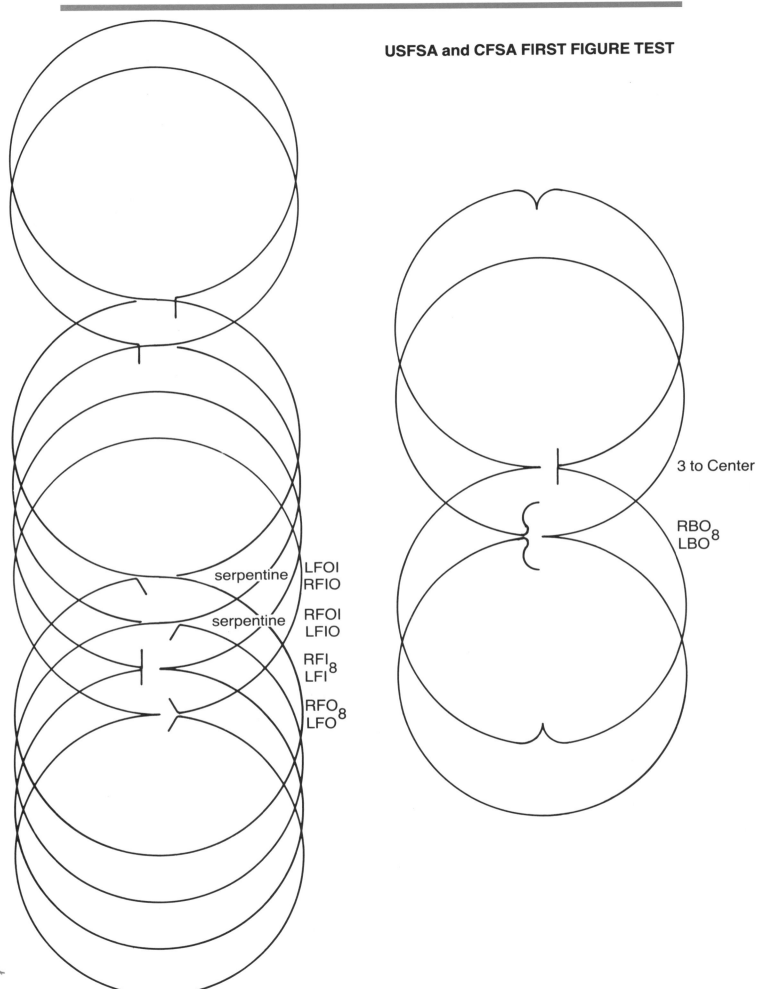

serpentine   LFOI
RFIO

serpentine   RFOI
LFIO

RFI_8
LFI^8

RFO_8
LFO^8

3 to Center

RBO_8
LBO^8

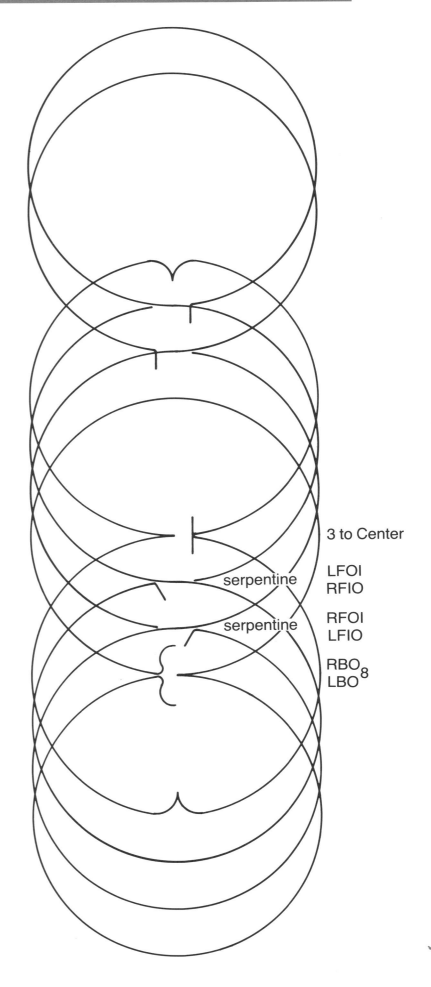

3 to Center

serpentine   LFOI
RFIO

serpentine   RFOI
LFIO

RBO $_8$
LBO

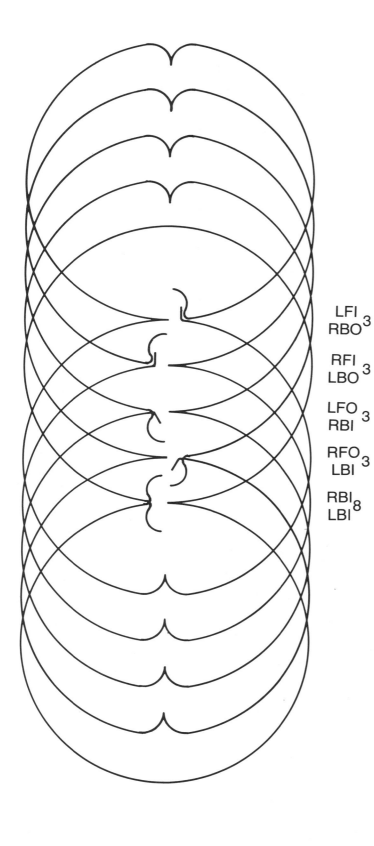

LFI $_3$
RBO

RFI $_3$
LBO

LFO $_3$
RBI

RFO $_3$
LBI

RBI $_8$
LBI

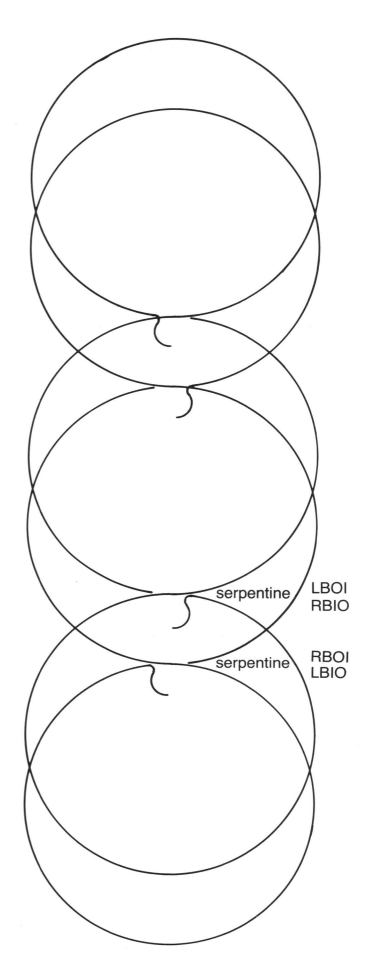

serpentine   LBOI
               RBIO

serpentine   RBOI
               LBIO

On this page draw a long axis and construct your test using the compass for each circle. Trace each figure 3 times on each circle, marking in the pushes and the turns. Check to see if you have maintained the same side line up and long axis on each figure.

Using your compass construct your test again on this page but without a long axis.

Now it's time to draw your whole test freehand WITHOUT your compass. Give it a try. Don't hesitate to make corrections to your circles as you draw the second and third tracings. When you are done compare it to the drawing of your test at the beginning of this chapter.

Draw your test one last time without your compass on this page. Feel proud of the work you have done!

Congratulations you are done! You've completed the FIGURE IT OUT! workbook. In honor of this achievement we will send you a diploma. All you have to do is send us your final drawing and the certification from your coach that you have completed the exercises in this book. You'll find a form in the middle of this page; just tear it out, present it to your coach, and then mail it to the following address:

Professional Skaters Guild of America
P.O. Box 5904
Rochester, MN 55903

We'll send a diploma to you as soon as possible!

COACH CERTIFICATION FORM

Skaters' Name _____

Street _____

City _____ State or Province _____ Zip Code _____

Country _____ Age _____

As the coach of _____ I certify that he/she has completed all 13 lessons of *FIGURE IT OUT*. Having successfully completed the *FIGURE IT OUT* program, please send this graduate a well deserved diploma.

Coach's Signature _____ Date _____

Rink _____ Skating Club _____

NEW ERA FIGURES

New Era Figures are an innovative figure system that has the support of the PSGA and its Board of Directors.

The figures, developed by Robert Ogilvie, use a combination of "New Era" figures, the "Richardson's Star Test" figures and the ISU figures.

If you are interested in purchasing a complete manual on New Era Figures, please send a check for $7.00 to NEF, PSGA, P.O. Box 5904, Rochester, MN 55903.